P9-CFP-744

The Sea for Breakfast

OTHER BOOKS BY LILLIAN BECKWITH
IN COMMON READER EDITIONS:

The Hills is Lonely
The Loud Halo

The Sea for Breakfast

LILLIAN BECKWITH

A COMMON READER EDITION
THE AKADINE PRESS

To:
'Bonny', 'Beauty', 'Bella'
& 'Blanche',
my four wild Highlanders.

The Sea for Breakfast

A COMMON READER EDITION published 1998
by The Akadine Press, Inc., by arrangement with the author.

Copyright © 1961 by Lillian Beckwith.
Copyright renewed © 1989 by Lillian Comber.

All rights reserved. No part of this publication may be
reproduced or transmitted in any form or by any means electronic
or mechanical, including photocopying, recording, or any other
information retrieval system, without permission in writing from
The Akadine Press, Inc., 141 Tompkins Avenue, Pleasantville,
New York 10570. Telephone 1-800-832-7323.

A COMMON READER EDITION and fountain colophon are
trademarks of The Akadine Press, Inc.

ISBN 1-888173-49-1

2 4 6 8 10 9 7 5 3 1

Contents

The characters in this book
are not intended to be those
of any living persons.

The Sea for Breakfast

I.   *A Place of My Own*

ONE HUNDRED AND TEN; one hundred and eleven, ouch!
One hundred and twelve, damn! For the third torrid day in
succession I was exasperatedly discovering and extracting
nails of every tortured shape and unexpected size from the
wooden walls of my cottage kitchen. My tool, which I had
previously understood to be a claw-headed hammer, had
been bestowed upon me by Ruari, the imperiously obliging brother of my former landlady. He however had referred to it more colourfully as a 'cloven-footed' hammer.
It was a typically Hebridean tool with a thick, rough handle
and a rusty head so loose on the shaft that it was a toss-up
each time whether the nail would be prised out of the wall,
or whether the 'cloven-foot' would remain poised vacillat-
ingly on the firmly embedded nail while I reeled back, brandishing the handle and recovering myself just in time to

receive a blow of acknowledgement from the descending head. For the umpteenth time I stopped to massage tingling elbows with grazed fingers and swore as I jammed the head savagely back on to the shaft. For the umpteenth time I wished, rather half-heartedly, that the little village of Bruach were not set amidst such glorious isolation and, most whole-heartedly, that the terrain were less abundantly provided with handy-sized stones. As it was, even this poor makeshift had necessitated some diligent seeking. Still, I comforted myself as I doggedly counted my successes (simply so as to prove just how many nails one may expect to find in an old croft kitchen), the unpredictability of proceedings did serve to enliven a task that otherwise might have been as soporific as counting sheep.

Just why any household should have wanted or needed more than a hundred nails disfiguring their kitchen I could not understand. The six-inch ones higher up on the walls and the ones in the rafters would of course have been used for hanging fishing nets. In addition to those serving as picture hooks and those used for hanging coats and oilskins, some of the rest would doubtless have been used for strings of salt fish or rabbit skins. A few dozen nails, even fifty, I would have been prepared to accept as a normal complement, but over a hundred!

'My kitchen walls,' I lamented to Morag after my first impact with them, 'have more nails to the square foot than a fakir's bed.'

'Aye, but those is Hamish's men's nails,' she replied reverently, and seeing that I looked blank, continued: 'Ach well,

4

mo ghaoil, d'you see, Hamish and Mary that lived there had seven sons and all of them men y'understand? Not like the wee ticks of things we have nowadays, but big men they was and strong, and every time one of them got back from the hill or from the sea they'd likely have a rabbit or a few fish and maybe a skart and they'd be after pickin' up a stone just and bangin' a nail into the wall so as to hang it away from the cats and the dogs.'

'It still puzzles me why there should have been such a glut of nails all ready to hand, here in Bruach of all places,' I said.

'But isn't the wood you gather from the shore full of them just, lassie? Have you no seen that for yourself? And Hamish's men wouldn't be the kind to be wastin' them.'

Thus was the plethora of nails explained. Now I should like to explain why I, during three picnic-perfect days of early June when cuckoos were yodelling across the sun-soaked moors and bluebells were pealing wildly into bloom, should be gloomily and resentfully pulling all Hamish's men's nails out again.

When her nephew in Glasgow had been involved in an accident which was supposed to have affected his health generally, Morag, the crofter landlady from whom I had rented half a house since my arrival in Bruach three years previously, had decided that he and his wife, who was herself a semi-invalid, should come to live with her on the croft where she could keep a strict eye on the two of them. She also, she said, intended to keep a strict eye on their precocious little daughter, a design which I suspected privately, having met the child, would result in her having one more subject for her tyranny, for Morag, like all Gaels, loved to have a child about the house to indulge. Naturally the new arrangement meant that Morag and I, to our mutual regret, must part company, and I was faced with the alternative of returning South or looking for other accommodation locally. After three years of crofting life and with ill health only a memory, I found I did not relish the idea of returning to the noisy clutter of life in England where nowadays it seems there is too much prosperity for real happiness; too much hurry for humour. In Bruach there was prosperity enough for most things and time mattered little. My days were pleasant and full and the nights brought unbroken sleep so that even dreams had the continuity of one long novel in contrast to the disjointedness of a book of short stories. And undoubtedly I had grown fond of Bruach and its inhabitants, for the Gaels of the Hebrides are indeed a happy race. Even their language is happy; listening to the Gaelic is like listening to a series of chuckles; there is always a lilt even in harangue; often a smile in a scold. I might be shocked at some of the events of the day, but at night I could chuckle myself to sleep over them. I wanted to stay in Bruach, so I looked for a place of my own.

There were two empty cottages not far from the village. 'Tigh-na-Craig' (House on the Rock), to the north, was situated close to the burial ground, the other, with an unpronounceable name—the nearest I could get to it was 'Tigh-na-Mushroomac'—to the south, adjoined the cleg-infested moor. Faced with a choice between clegs and corpses I chose the clegs and was immensely relieved I had done so when I later heard Erchy, the poacher, telling someone: 'Ach, the grave will no take long to dig. It's no a County Council burial ground so you'll not have to go more than two feet. It's no trouble at all.' The County apparently insisted on four feet.

The cottage of 'Tigh-na-Mushroomac' had been empty when I had first arrived in Bruach but the fact that it might be for sale did not emerge until after I had announced my intention of settling. The Bruachites are averse to putting their property on the open market but like to be wooed into graciously permitting you to buy provided you can convince them of your need and of your bank balance. Callum, one of Hamish's surviving sons and the owner of the cottage, lived in Glasgow, so I lost no time in contacting him and in visiting the local policeman in whose charge the key had been left.

My first meeting with the policeman, soon after my arrival in Bruach, had left a distinctly droll impression on both our minds. I had been on my way back to Morag's one drearily wet evening when I had come upon his car parked plumb in the centre of the road, without lights of any sort. A little farther along the road a lorry too was stopped and beside it the policeman, watched attentively by the lorry driver, was siphoning petrol out of the tank of the lorry into a can. When he had transferred the petrol to the tank of his own car, the policeman generously offered me a lift home. Morag had been away in Glasgow at the time and as the policeman had yet to finish the enquiries about poaching he was engaged on making in the village, I invited him in for a meal. Earlier in the day Erchy had handed me a parcel of fish which he had said offhandedly were mackerel. I cooked one for the policeman. Before the meal he had seemed much dispirited by the results of his day's work, but after the fish and several cups of tea his geniality was restored. Indeed he became quite jovial. He complimented me on my cooking and when he got up to go he impressed upon me that I must be very sure to thank Erchy for him and tell him that he, the policeman, had 'never tasted mackerel like them'. I assured him I would do so.

'He said what?' demanded Erchy when I had innocently kept my promise.

'He asked me to tell you he'd never tasted mackerel so good,' I repeated.

'Damty sure he hasn't,' muttered Erchy, turning a little pale. 'Why the Hell did you want to let him see them?'

'But you told me they were mackerel. Weren't they?'

'Mackerel indeed! D'you mean to say you can't tell the difference between what's a trout and what's a mackerel? And do you not know trout's illegal?'

At that stage of my initiation I was incapable of distinguishing a legal fish from an illegal one, having hitherto relied on my fishmonger to identify my fish for me. Full of contrition, I admitted my defections.

Erchy stared at me with both pity and amazement. 'Sometimes,' he said crushingly, 'I think school teachers is the most ignorantest people out.'

Since that episode one of the policeman's eyes had always drooped into an indubitable wink whenever we had met and now that I approached him with a request for the key of 'Tigh-na-Mushroomac' he appeared to find it excessively funny.

'You're thinkin' of buyin' "Tigh-na-Mushroomac", are you? Well, right enough I did have the key once but I've lost it now. Indeed, when the door was blown in by the storm a year or two back the only way I could keep it shut again was to ram a big stone behind it and tie a good piece of string to it. You'll see the string under the door. You'll pull it towards you when you come out and it rolls and jams the door. Keeps it closed better than the old lock that was on it before, I'm tellin' you.' He was so taken with his contrivance that it seemed a pity to draw his attention to the fact that I must first get into the cottage. 'Ach, you'll give it a good shove just. Mind now, it'll need to be a right good one, for it's a biggish stone. You'd best get one of the lads to do it for you,' he added on second thoughts.

It was a grey day with sneaky little flurries of wind which dashed us sporadically with chilly drops of rain when Morag and I went to pay our first visit of inspection. Morag had enlisted for me the help of Peter, the son of Sheena, who worked the croft adjoining 'Tigh-na-Mushroomac'. Peter was a doughty, chrysanthemum-headed youth whose shape suggested that his mother had placed a heavy weight on his head in childhood to make him grow broad rather than long. When he smiled his wide gummy smile it looked as though someone had cut his throat. When he laughed he looked as though he was going to come to pieces. He now strode beside us along the shingle track, his shoulder hunched as though in eager preparation for the assault on the door.

'My,' confided Morag with a little shudder, 'I don't like the look of him at all. He looks that wild.' I glanced surreptitiously at Peter, who was wearing such a ridiculously tight pair of trousers and such a constraining jersey that it looked impossible for him to be anything but extremely well disciplined. 'And he's that lonely,' went on Morag steadily as she assessed the baby hill and the bare half mile of road that separated 'Tigh-na-Mushroomac' from the rest of the houses, 'you'll have none but the sheeps for company.'

I told her, patiently, for I had told her many times, that I did not mind the solitude.

'But, mo ghaoil,' she argued, 'you could die here and none of us the wiser till the butcher smelled you out.'

Built of grey stone, 'Tigh-na-Mushroomac' squatted in smug solitude at the extreme tip of Bruach bay, its two lower windows like dark secrets half buried in the three-foot thick walls. From the sloping felt roof two tiny dormer windows peeped inquisitively at the sea which at high tide skirmished no more than twenty yards away. In fact it would not have needed an unduly exaggerated fishing rod to have enabled one to lean from one's bedroom window and draw upon the sea for breakfast each morning.

Behind the cottage was the neglected croft which merged into the wildness of the moors and they in their turn stretched to prostrate themselves at the feet of the lonely hills. It would have been cruel to have insisted to Morag that its distance from the rest of the houses was, for me, one of 'Tigh-na-Mushroomac's' chief attractions. The Gaels as a general rule seem to have no desire for privacy, building their houses as close to one another as croft boundaries will permit. 'Alone-ness' is a state they cannot endure and 'any company is better than no company' is a maxim that is accepted literally whether the company be that of an idiot or a corpse. Not desiring it for themselves, they can neither understand nor really believe in the desire of other people for privacy and so genuinely anxious are they that you should not be lonely they continually seek you out of your cherished solitude.

Outside the cottage Peter turned on us his cut-throat grin and poised himself ready for action.

'All right now, Peter,' said Morag. 'I'll lift the sneck.' Peter rammed his shoulder fiercely into the door; there was a short, sharp protest from the rusty hinges as they parted company with the wood; the door fell inwards, see-sawed across the big stone so thoughtfully provided by the policeman, and flung Peter into the farthest corner of the porch. Bewilderedly Peter picked himself up, revealing that he now had two long, gaping splits in the seat of his trousers.

'Peter!' upbraided Morag, blushing for his predicament. 'You've broken your trousers!' Peter looked somewhat puzzled and felt each of his limbs in turn but thus reassured he became more concerned with locating a splinter which, he said, had 'come out and lost itself on him'. I diplomatically went upstairs and minutes later heard his exclamations of relief and then his dismissal by Morag. Through a bedroom window I caught sight of his stocky figure fleeing homewards across the moors, presumably minus his splinter and with his rear parts effectively camouflaged by Morag's best floral silk apron which she had fortunately been wearing beneath her coat. My landlady joined me upstairs.

'Didn't I tell Sheena this mornin' just,' said Morag complacently, 'that Peter was gettin' too tight for his trousers?'

Inside, 'Tigh-na-Mushroomac' was a replica of all the two-storeyed croft cottages I had seen, there being a kitchen leading off one side of the entrance porch and 'the room' off the other. In Bruach this second room was never known as anything but 'the room', presumably because no one was really sure of its intended purpose. Morag, in her original letter to me had described hers as 'the room that wasn't a kitchen'. Usually the anonymous room was necessary as a bedroom and indeed in many of the single-storeyed croft houses these two rooms, with a recessed bed in the kitchen, comprised the whole of the living accommodation. Yet in such limited space large families were reared and a galaxy of scholars produced. It was no unusual sight to see a university student at his books by the light of a candle in a corner of the small kitchen, while all around him the neighbours jostled and gossiped, argued and sang. Neither was it unusual in due course to see that student's name high in the list of honours graduates.

'Tigh-na-Mushroomac' provided ample accommodation for a spinster. It had two rooms upstairs and, though these were of attic proportions with the windows at floor level so that one had to sit down on the floor to look out through them, they were habitable. The cottage needed a certain amount of repair; first on the list was a new front door. But its walls and its roof were sound. I liked what I saw.

It seemed to me that everyone in the village took a hand in the ensuing transaction, and when it came to bargaining they ranged themselves with complete affability either on the side of Callum or myself, or, with true Gaelic adroitness on the side of both parties. With so many cooks the broth should have been irrevocably spoiled but eventually everything was settled to everyone's complete satisfaction and I became the delighted owner of a cottage and croft.

As I could afford only the minimum number of alterations to begin with, I decided that priority must be given to getting larger windows put in the kitchen and 'the room'. I wanted snugness but not permanent twilight in my new home.

'But, mo ghaoil, think how they'll show up the dust,' warned Sheena, who had lived all her life in a dark, thatched cottage and whose only use for a duster was to wipe over a chair whenever a visitor accepted the hospitality of her kitchen; a necessary precaution, considering a hen had most likely been the former occupant.

Erchy, with whom I consulted, startled me by admitting that he 'quite liked a bit of work now and then just as a change when he could spare the time', and by promptly agreeing to undertake the task. True to his word he was soon at work taking out the old frames and enlarging the window space. When he had got thus far there was a lull in his activities.

'What's happened to Erchy these days?' I asked at a ceilidh one night. 'He seems to have gone on strike. There's been no work done on my cottage for days.'

'Oh, he'll not be workin' at anythin' for a week yet,' explained Johnny. 'He's got his girl friend from Glasgow stayin' in the village and they're away every night to the heather.'

'That's not his girl friend,' contradicted Morag indignantly.

'Maybe not,' conceded Johnny easily, 'but he'll make do with her while she's here.'

But the return of Erchy's proxy girl friend to Glasgow did not, unfortunately, result in a resumption of activity by Erchy. A wedding was announced at which he was to act as best man. Erchy got drunk in anticipation, drunk for the solemnization and drunk again in recollection. A week later there was a dance and Erchy got drunk in preparation. He reckoned he'd never have the courage to ask a girl to dance with him if he was sober. A cattle sale followed closely on the heels of the dance and Erchy's beasts made the highest prices; he stayed drunk for nearly a week! By this time winter was upon us and Noachian deluges, lashed by fierce gales, washed the exposed room inside and out. Hailstones pitted the wood-lined walls; spiders' webs were torn from their anchorages; salt spray filmed the floors. It was on a particularly savage day, with a full-blooded gale inverting the waterfalls over the cliffs and sending them billowing skywards, that I went over to the cottage to reassure myself that it was still there. Hungry green breakers were hurling themselves at the shingle shore, flinging spume high over the roof of 'Tigh-na-Mushroomac'. The wind seemed to have chosen the poor little cottage as its main target and I was buffeted towards it. Inside I found Erchy frenziedly prising out the small window from the back of the kitchen.

'My, but it's coarse, coarse weather,' he announced.

'Erchy!' I yelled, ignoring the greeting in the belief that he was still suffering from the effects of his recent orgies. 'I don't want that window out, you idiot!'

'I canna' get it open,' Erchy yelled back. 'I've got to try will I get it out. It can go back when it's needed.'

'It's needed now if ever it was,' I retorted savagely.

'My God, woman!' Erchy shouted at me above the storm. 'Do you not know that where the wind gets in it's got to get out again? If you don't let it out here you'll lose your roof. Wind's the same in a house as it is in a stomach; you've got to let it blow its way out once it's in. You canna trap wind.'

I watched him dubiously, slowly becoming aware that not only was the floor pulsing as though there were an engine beneath my feet, but that interspersed with the noise of the storm were strained creakings and groanings from the timbers of the ceiling.

'This floor's quaking,' I said tensely.

'You are yourself too, I dare say,' retorted Erchy unrelentingly. 'And if you had this amount of wind under your beams you'd be quaking a lot worse.' I subsided into the most sheltered corner of the kitchen. 'Hear that now?' Erchy continued as an ominous thudding became audible from somewhere above. I listened; it sounded as though the ceiling joists were stamping against the walls in their impatience to be gone. 'That should stop when I get this clear.' He wrenched the window free and lowered it to the comparative shelter of the ground outside. 'Now listen!' he commanded, but though I listened obediently I was not much the wiser. The whole cottage seemed to be threatening to take wing at any moment. 'Aye, you'd have lost your roof all right tonight, I doubt,' said Erchy with great satisfaction.

Through interminable weeks 'Tigh-na-Mushroomac' waited, naked and exposed, for the new door and windows to arrive. Glass, I was told, was scarce and when at last it was obtainable the mid-winter gales followed, one after another, so that the carrier complained it was impossible for him to get across to the mainland. A brief respite from the gales brought the snow, which blocked the road. Blessedly came the thaw—which washed the road away. A day of calm dawned; there was no snow and the road had been repaired. With bated breath I telephoned the carrier.

'Oh, indeed I'm sorry but the tide's not just in the right state for loadin' at the pier,' he said with practised apology. 'Not till next week it won't be.'

Next week brought a repetition of the previous delays but when the tide had crept round again to a suitable state and miraculously it coincided with a period of calm I again 'phoned the carrier.

'Did you no hear, Miss Peckwitt?' he answered plaintively. 'My lorry broke on Monday and I've no managed to get it sorted yet. I canna' say when I'll be out now.'

Every time I visited my refrigerated little cottage I became a little more despondent. Every night I prayed the Almighty for patience. But the day did come when the elements acted in unison and nothing 'broke' and the carrier's lorry came romping along the track to the cottage to deliver two beautiful new windows and one front door. The front door was not new. There was a little note from the merchant explaining that he had not been able to procure a new door of the right size so he had taken the liberty of sending this one which had been removed from the local police station. He hoped I wouldn't mind! The carrier had also brought cans of paint, rolls of paper and turps, so whilst Erchy set to work installing the windows, I began to paper 'the room'. The original colour of the walls of 'the room' was really indescribable and the nearest I came to identifying it was in the recollection of a time when Morag, suspecting her calf was sick, was debating with me whether or not she should send for the vet.

'What makes you think there's something wrong with him?' I had asked as we watched the beast skipping around on his tether. 'He looks healthy enough to me.'

'Aye,' Morag had agreed reluctantly, 'he looks all right in himself but see now,' she had explained, indicating his smeared rump, 'his dung is such an unhappy colour.'

Once the windows had been put in I installed a camp bed and a couple of borrowed chairs and one or two other essentials and moved into the cottage. A few nights afterwards four of the girls from the village turned up to inspect progress. My spirits sank a little, for where the girls went soon the men would follow and then there would be a ceilidh and I would have to stop work and provide tea. I told them I was just planning to start papering upstairs. 'We'll give you a hand,' they volunteered. My spirits sank lower. As I expected, it was not long before some of the lads were bursting in, completely sure of their welcome and, giving up any thought of doing more work, I prepared to settle down for an evening's ceilidh, hoping the girls would forget their offer of help. The prospect of a wasted evening was not nearly so discomposing as the prospect of having to accept their help with the decorating.

'Come on,' said Dollac, the village beauty, inexorably. 'We're all goin' to help Miss Peckwitt paint and paper upstairs so she can have it all ready for a good ceilidh. Get the paint, you Ally. Is the paper cut? Those that can't do paintin' or paperin' can do some scrapin'.' Feebly I tried to dissuade them. 'Now just you get on with finishing the room,' they told me. I submitted to the juggernaut of their enthusiasm and when I had put the last few touches to 'the room', I carried water from the well and coaxed the stove into heating it. I found biscuits and collected odd cups and mugs, since my own crockery had not yet arrived. As I worked there came from above bursts of song, the banging of doors, clanging of paint cans, uninhibited shrieks, yells of tension, thudding of feet and generally such a hullabaloo that I doubted if ever I should be able to clean up their mess in anything short of a decade.

'Tea!' I called up the stairs and there was such an im-

mediate scatteration that I fully expected a brace of paint
cans to come hurtling down the stairs too. My helpers had
enjoyed themselves immensely; that at least was obvious.
Each one of them had a swipe of paint across a cheek, a
decoration which Dollac dismissed as being the result of a
game of 'paint-brush tag'—to see who would get the most
paint on him. When they had finished their tea and biscuits they rampaged back upstairs to 'finish things off'. I
felt that the phrase would turn out to be most appropriate.
I heated more water and washed the cups, envisaging myself having to take time off from cleaning up the farrago in
order to go to the post office to 'phone for a large supply of
paint remover and a repeat order for paint and wallpaper.
It was the early hours of the morning before my helpers
came trooping down the stairs again. They had cleaned the
paint off their faces and I wondered vaguely how and where.
They had finished both bedrooms, they said, and they were
'beautiful just', but they must have my promise not to go
upstairs and look at them until after breakfast. They
wouldn't look so good until then, they explained, because
there were still some wet patches; I must wait to inspect it
until it was all properly dry. The promise was an easy one
to make for I felt much too debilitated then to climb the
stairs and face up to the chaos which I was certain would
confront me. Yet, after breakfast, when I felt strong enough
to bear the sight of it all, I went upstairs and found there
was no chaos at all; I could not have hoped to have done
the job nearly so well myself. The unused materials were
stacked tidily in a corner, and paint splashes had been

cleaned away. It was, as they had said, beautiful—beautiful just. But only Gaels, I believe, could have accomplished such a splendid job and yet have derived so much fun and frolic from doing it.

The following night the volunteers turned up again but now there remained only the kitchen to be decorated and as I insisted that all the nails should come out first and as no more tools were procurable the evening's work degenerated into a cosy ceilidh. And that is why on this hot June day I came to be pulling out my one hundred and twenty-third nail when I heard the voice of Sheena, Peter's mother, hailing me from the door.

'My, but you're a hardy!'

I gathered up my harvest of nails from a chair and pushed on the kettle. In Bruach no work was ever considered too pressing to neglect hospitality and the arrival of the most casual visitor automatically ensured the popping on of the kettle.

'I've taken a hundred-and-twenty-three nails out of this kitchen so far,' I told Sheena, 'and I believe there are still one or two left.'

'Oh aye,' she replied. 'But Hamish was always such a handy man. Mary had never but to ask for a nail and he'd have it in for her. Aye, a right handy man he was.'

'I'm not nearly so handy at pulling them out,' I said ruefully.

'No, but why go to the trouble mo ghaoil? You'll surely want to hang things yourself and you'll be glad of a nail here and there.'

'Not a hundred-and-twenty-three times,' I said.

'No, maybe,' she admitted. 'But there's pictures.' (I should mention that the kitchen was about twelve feet by ten feet and no more than seven feet high.) 'And will you no need a nail for your girdle?' In Bruach a girdle is something a woman bakes on—not something she steps into. 'And then you never know but what you might want to dry a rabbit skin or two, and a few fish maybe.' I hoped I never should. 'You'll need some for towels some place and a corkscrew . . .' she was enumerating enthusiastically now; 'and a holder for your kettle and a couple of calendars and a wee bunch of feathers for the hearth. You have no man,' she giggled, 'so you'll no be needin' nails for him. Men needs an awful lot of nails in a house,' she told me. 'You must see and keep some, mo ghaoil, surely.'

I surveyed my rusty harvest. I'd be dammed if any of them were going back in again, I decided, and between sips of tea Sheena sighed for my improvidence.

'My, but your new windows are beautiful just,' she enthused, slewing round her chair so that she could stare out at the sea. The windows had made an enormous difference to the cottage, giving a wide view of the bay which today was full of sunshine and silver-flecked water. On the shore, sandpipers scurried busily in the shingle and serenaded the quiescent ripples while thrift danced to the music of the sea. Above the outer islands comically shaped clouds, like assorted carnival hats, were strewn haphazardly across the sky. The black hills lay in a drugged haze, Garbh Bienn looking like an old man who has fallen peacefully asleep in

21

his chair; the wisp of white cloud across its middle like the newspaper fallen from his face.

'You know,' said Sheena, whose appreciation of nature was purely gastronomical, 'this weather ought to bring the mackerel in.'

She finished her tea and as she got up to go she remembered she had a telegram for me in her pocket. 'I was passin' the post office and NellyElly said would I bring it. It's only to tell you your furniture's comin' next Tuesday.'

Sheena had only been gone a few minutes when Morag arrived and we were soon joined by Erchy who had been painting his dinghy down on the shore. The kettle had to go on again. I begrudged no one tea and I had grown tolerant of time-wasting, but I was plagued by the fact that water for every purpose had to be carried from a well over a hundred yards away down on the shore, which meant that I had to struggle uphill with the full pails. It was aggravating to have to squelch about the croft in gumboots even during a prolonged drought and to realize that though there was an excess of water everywhere it was too undisciplined to be of use to me. I was ironically reminded of my own mother's injunction, 'Don't leave the kettle boiling, wasting gas'; here I had to remind myself; 'Don't leave the kettle boiling, wasting water'. With so much cleaning to do the carrying of water was proving a strength-sapping business and I was very anxious to get the guttering of the cottage replaced so that I could have rainwater for household purposes. The guttering, along with a rainwater tank, had been on order for many weeks and Morag brought news of it now.

'She's on her way,' Morag announced triumphantly 'You'll not want for water when she comes.'

'You're not telling me that my rainwater tank is on its way at last, are you?' I asked hopefully.

'Yes, indeed. I saw the carrier yesterday just and he told me to tell you that if the Lord spares him he'll be out with her tomorrow for certain.'

'That will be a blessing,' I said. However, as I pointed out, the new tank would not overcome the drinking water problem because I had discovered that when there was a combination of high tide and a strong wind the sea came into my well so that the water was decidedly brackish some-times.

'So it will be, mo ghaoil,' Morag agreed. 'But you know the old doctor who was here always used to tell us that if everybody took a good drink of plain sea-water once a week there'd not be so many sore stomachs goin' around.'

'That may be true, but I don't like salty tea,' I demurred. 'I rather wish I could get hold of one of those water divin-ers to come and find me a nice convenient well here on the croft.'

'Them fellows,' said Morag contemptuously; 'they had one hereabouts a long time back to try would he find a corpse in the hills and a few folks was sayin' we ought to let him try would he find more wells for us here in Bruach.'

'What happened?'

'Oh, they let him try all right, and he said there was water here and there was water there, and my fine fellow took ten shillings from each of us for sayin' so, but when folks started digging they found it was drier underneath than it was up at the top. They'd lost their money and they'd found no water.'

'They didn't go deep enough,' put in Erchy, with a wink at me.

'Indeed they did. He said there was water on our own Ruari's croft at twenty feet and Ruari dug down until we could see only the cap of him just, sticking out of the top of the hole he'd made and still there was no water. Ach, I'm no believin' in them fellows at all. Maybe they can find corpses but I doubt they canna' find water.' It struck me then as strange that the Bruachites, who genuinely believe in and often claim to be gifted with the second sight, should yet be so sceptical of water divining. I recollected that I had never heard of a Hebridean water diviner.

'What you'll have to do, my dear,' went on Morag, 'is to drink the wild water.'

'The wild water?' I echoed.

'Aye, what you catch from your roof.'

'For drinking?' I grimaced, thinking of all the dear little birds I heard scratching and sliding on my roof every morning; of the starlings fumigating themselves around the chimney and the gulls daily parading the length of the ridging. Morag laughed.

'You'll soon get used to that, lassie,' she predicted firmly. And she was right.

She watched me take out the last half-score or so of nails, giving a grunt of 'there now!' at each success.

'Anybody would think it was you doin' the work,' Erchy

told her.

'If you was half as good as the men who put in the nails you'd be after takin' them out for Miss Peckwitt instead of sittin' watchin' her,' she rebuked him.

Erchy drained his cup. When Morag was on the defensive her tongue could become caustic and he was ready to flee from it.

'D'you know you're wearin' odd shoes,' he taunted her.

'Ach, Erchy, but you know me. I just puts my feets into the first things that I pull from under the bed.'

'That could be damty awkward sometimes, I doubt,' he said as he disappeared homeward.

Morag watched me fill a pail with hot water and pour in some disinfectant.

'My,' she commented with an appreciative sniff, 'I do like this disinfectant you use. It has such a lovely flavour.'

While I washed down the walls she told me of the prowess of Hamish and his sons. They had, it seemed, all possessed Herculean strength, though, according to Morag, the sons had been no match for their father. She told me of the prodigious loads he could carry; of how he alone could lift to shoulder height the three stones at the entrance to the village by which every man coming home from the sales was accustomed, in days gone by, to test his strength; of how he could lift a boat that taxed the strength of four lesser men. She related with pride the stories of his skill in breaking horses; of how he used to walk all the way from Glasgow once every five years and, when he reached home, to show he was not tired, he used to leap over the garden gate. (I was less impressed with this latter feat, for if I had left Glasgow two hundred miles behind me I have no doubt I too should have felt like leaping a gate.)

'What are you goin' to name your cottage now that you have it ready?' she asked, draining her fourth cup of tea.

'Oh, I shan't bother to change it from "Tigh-na-Mushroomac",' I said. 'I must get the correct Gaelic spelling.'

'Here, but you mustn't call it that. Not on letters, anyway,' Morag said with a gasp.

'Why not?' I asked. 'What does it mean?'

'It doesn't suit it just. And it's no rightly a name at all. It's just what it's always been called since I can remember.'

'But, Morag, what does it mean?'

'Indeed I don't know,' she lied firmly. 'Erchy's mother says to tell you she has a wee poc of fish put by for you when you're passin' that way,' she continued hastily and made for the door.

It was of little use pressing Morag further, that I knew, and I walked with her as far as Erchy's, pondering on the meaning of 'Tigh-na-Mushroomac' and why it should be considered an unsuitable name to be put on letters. I recalled the excessive amusement of the policeman when he had learned I was thinking of buying the house and I wondered if it had been caused in some measure by the unsuitability of the name. I knew that in the Gaelic 'Tigh' means 'house', but never having seen the spelling of the name I could not identify the rest as being any Gaelic words I knew

'Erchy,' I demanded, 'what does "Tigh-na-

Mushroomac" mean?'

Erchy looked a long, long way out to sea, and his lips tightened to repress a smile. 'Don't you get feedin' any of that fish to the pollis,' he warned me, 'and if you meet him with it, run for your life.'

'How do you spell "Tigh-na-Mushroomac?"' I persisted, after a hasty glance at the fish which I could now recognize as being nothing more illicit than mackerel.

'Indeed, I don't know,' he replied with simulated apology.

His evasion strengthened my determination to find out so I put the question to an old scholar who loved his language and who was patient with those who might wish to learn it.

'Oh well, now, you mustn't call the house that,' he answered me smoothly. 'No, no, that wouldn't do at all. It's not really a name but just a description the village has always had for it. Go and tell Morag she must tell you the story of it. She's the best one to tell you, and you must tell her that from me.'

I thanked him and went again to Morag. She was washing dishes and when I told her why I had come she began scrutinizing each dish lingeringly to avoid meeting my eye.

'Well, mo ghaoil,' she began, with an embarrassed chuckle. 'It was Hamish's lads when they was younger. They wouldn't come out once they were in . . . y'understand?' She managed to give me an insinuating glance, and then plunged on with her story. It appeared that one or two of Hamish's less tractable sons had developed a dislike for work and so evaded it by disappearing into the 'wee hoosie' in the back garden where, immune to the threats and cajolery of their parents, they had stayed for long periods reading books or papers. Hamish had at last become so incensed that he had one day taken the saw and sawn the traditional round hole into a rough square one. The simplicity of his strategy was rivalled only by its effectiveness and, after enforced experience, I have no hesitation in recommending this form of torture to anyone who is barbaric enough to be interested in such practices. Inevitably, Hamish's family had come to be known in Bruach and beyond as the 'square bums' and their house as 'the house of square bums'.

Once acquainted with the story I lost no time in choosing for my cottage a name that I could unashamedly put on my letters. For the seat in the 'wee hoosie' I had already substituted one of more conventional shape.

II.   *Settling In*

WITH MY COTTAGE BRIGHTLY redecorated so that even the
unhappy walls of the 'room', now my bedroom, were laughing with warmth and colour, I was ready to receive my furniture which, as the telegram had said, was due to arrive
the following Tuesday. I very much wanted to pay a visit to
the mainland to buy one or two last-minute necessities and
as 'Joanna', the little second-hand car I had bought in England, was undergoing repairs, I planned to catch the bus on
Monday morning, do my shopping, stay the night and get
a lift back with the furniture lorry the following day. Everything worked according to plan except for one tense half-
hour when, with only a few minutes to spare before I was
due to meet the lorry, I darted into a telephone kiosk on
the station and was imprisoned as the result of a careless
lorry driver backing his lorry against the kiosk door and

going off for a cup of tea. It was an embarrassing and vexatious experience. People hurried by to the train, heedless of my gesticulations; they heard neither my calls nor my hammerings. When I did eventually manage to attract the attention of a couple of station loiterers they stared at me with mingled curiosity and trepidation before they would come near. When they realized what had happened they bolted off in search of the driver, believing no doubt that I was intending to catch the train which was due to leave in a few minutes' time; fortunately another loiterer waited long enough to listen to my plea for someone to go down to the pier and hold up the furniture lorry.

At the pier, where I arrived harassed and apologetic, the driver was as glad to see me as I was to see him. He had never been to the Island before, he told me, and he hadn't any idea of the road anyhow and he might have been driving around all day looking for the place. The two itinerant labourers, who had already been recruited to help with the unloading, tore themselves away from a knot of arguing fishermen and installed themselves in the back of the lorry and we set off. Weightily the lorry rumbled along the rutty roads with every now and then explosive comments from the driver on their condition and their sinuousness. Shepherds called in their dogs to heel while they stood and watched us impassively. Women, carrying water or moving tethered cows, stopped their work to wave and smile. At one isolated cottage which had a long view of the road, an old woman came hurrying out holding aloft a large jug of milk and some cups. The driver pulled up and taking a slopping cup of milk which she urged upon him, handed it to me. I drank obediently, and allowed the driver to drink his too, stifling the knowledge that conditions in the interior of the woman's home much belied its white-washed appearance and that of her batch of children several were patients in the mainland sanatorium. She would accept no payment. It gratified her to offer refreshment to passing strangers and our enjoyment of it was her reward. When we handed back the empty jug and the cups her maze of happy wrinkles deepened delightedly and her kind old face flushed with pleasure. She still stood there as we drove away, smiling, nodding her head and waving until we were out of sight.

The road now wound picturesquely around the head of the loch so that we had the full-skirted hills jostling us on one side and water lapping at our wheels on the other. The driver said, not inaptly, that he felt as though he was between the Devil and the deep blue sea, though the day was grey and the loch not blue but darkly reflective. The hill peaks loomed sinister through swirling clouds of mist which polished their craggy faces. Scenically it was awe-inspiring. The driver said it gave him the willies. He would have liked to accelerate and get away from it but the road made that impossible. He became noticeably less talkative.

I was preoccupied with the problem of how to arrange my various possessions in the cottage and was already experiencing the thrill of once again handling some of the dear, familiar things which I knew were stored in the back of the lorry: the silver model of 'The Olde Curiosity Shoppe'; the white Grecian urn that would be the perfect setting for the large sprays of rowanberries in their season; my set of Cézanne prints. . . . The lorry came to an abrupt stop. I looked at the driver questioningly. He was staring aghast at the little wooden bridge spanning the burn which surged and rumbled over the green-grey rocks into the loch.

'I'm not taking this lorry over that thing,' he said flatly.

I was appalled. I had to admit the fragile appearance of the bridge and recalled that when I had first travelled the Bruach road I had had serious doubts about its suitability for anything but the lightest of vehicular traffic. Since then I had seen loaded lorries, buses and even a steam roller negotiate it with absolute safety. There was a thumping from the back of the lorry and in a moment the two recruits appeared beside the cab. They looked at the bridge suspiciously and agreed with the driver that it didn't look safe.

'The bus goes over it regularly,' I said brightly. 'And coal lorries with a couple of tons of coal.'

The driver shook his head.

I visualized myself and my furniture being abandoned beside the loch miles from Bruach. I wondered what on earth I should do.

'Well,' volunteered one of the men, 'you canna' turn round and go back, there's nowhere to turn.'

Thank God for that, I thought.

The driver looked momentarily panic-stricken. The two men walked along to the bridge and tried jumping up and down on it, cautiously at first and then with growing confidence. The driver decided to go and inspect it for himself and soon all three of them were trotting up and down the bridge with serious concentration.

'It takes a lot of heavy traffic,' I called out.

'Aye?'

'Aye!' I confirmed.

The driver came back. 'I can try it,' he said timorously.

'Wait now,' commanded one of the men, pointing to one of the smaller struts of the bridge. 'This piece is broken.' He pulled a piece of parcel string out of his pocket and painstakingly tied the two halves of the strut together. When that was accomplished he waved the waiting lorry forward.

'We'll walk across,' they offered magnanimously, 'that'll lighten the load.'

'Aye?' agreed the driver dubiously.

Their apprehension had its effect on me and I too climbed down from the lorry.

'Every little helps,' I comforted treacherously.

With stiff-faced pessimism the driver inched the quaking lorry across the bridge, his relief on reaching the other side showing itself in a little burst of speed that sent an exultant spatter of gravel and dust up from its tyres. He waited for us to get back in, but first I ran back to the bridge. I had a camera with me and under the pretext of taking a photograph of the burn I focused it on the string-tied strut. I still have that photograph. It shows plainly the two halves of the strut bound firmly together—the string is tied in a lover's knot!

There was a covey of Bruachites at the cottage to unload the van and after a couple of hours of heavings, pushings, questionings and teasings the furniture was installed and we were waving good-bye to the driver and his men who, much impressed by the repeated assurances of the villagers as to the enormous loads carried over the little wooden bridge and fortified by a tip and a couple of drams of whisky apiece, seemed not at all dismayed by the prospect of the return journey.

It was some days later that Morag, who had devoted much of her time to helping me straighten things out, sat with me in the kitchen drinking tea. 'Everywhere looks beautiful just,' she murmured happily, 'and so tastily furnished,' she added, looking as though she might at any moment take a bite out of the settee. I was really quite taken with the way things were looking myself. 'Now that you're near settled and you've got your gramophone, you'll have to give a party,' she said.

'I'd already thought of that,' I said. 'I'll have to ask the grocer if he can get me some drinks. I used up the last of mine on the removal men.'

'Oh, you'll not get whisky from him, mo ghaoil,' she informed me flatly. 'He hasn't got an explosives licence.'

Though there was still a certain amount of renovation needed inside the cottage I had to abandon work on it temporarily so that I could start cutting a supply of peats for the winter. Peat was still the main fuel used in Bruach though all but a few diehards were beginning to use coal in addition to the peats which their deep old-fashioned grates consumed ravenously. Coal supplies, however, were erratic and depended very much upon the caprice and commitments of the undertaker who ran the business of coal merchant as a sideline and who seemed to think it would be as indelicate to offer a ton of coal before it was needed as it would be to offer a coffin. Any order for less than a ton per household he would decline arrogantly, even when rationing elsewhere was at its strictest, and not until he had collected firm orders for the minimum number of tons needed to coax a coal boat from the safety of a Glasgow wharf would he dispatch the order. Weeks later, when a sufficiently derelict puffer, looking as though the only reason it had managed to make the trip was because it was trying to run away from itself, came chugging and wallowing its laden way to the Island pier, the undertaker would hastily enlist volunteers and croft work would be neglected while the men went off to unload. The coal was tipped in half-ton scoopfuls straight from the boat into lorries which then took it to the consumers, the different tons being separated by odd bits of cardboard or sacking which would of course be blown away or shaken down among the coal before the lorry had gone more than a mile or two. The unloading of a 'puffer' was always a merry affair with Gaelic oaths and jests flying about as thickly as the coal dust itself. It was a regular practice of the men to try to fling one another's caps into the lorry just at the moment the coal was being tipped in and there was much mirth both at the dispatching and receiving ends when this was successfully accomplished. But the trophies one might discover in one's coal were not confined to caps: as the same pier was used for unloading coal as for unloading fish, it was not at all unusual to find fish hooks, fish heads, bits of seaweed and crab claws on one's shovel; though the fact that after some stoking one's kitchen became redolent of a guano factory was more often the result of the loaded lorries having to pass through a passage-way locally termed 'bomb alley', where hundreds of gorged seagulls wheeled in ecstasy and extruded indiscriminately. When unloading was completed the volunteers, black all over, would return home to clean themselves up and to have their clothes well sprinkled with the louse powder they used for the cattle. The Bruachites maintained that coal was full of fleas and houses close to the pier were said to become infested whenever a coal boat was unloading.

Thus was one's supply of fuel obtained and the disadvantage was that if one had ordered a couple of tons or so and it turned out to be of poor quality then one was stuck with it. I discovered this for myself the very first time I took a delivery of coal—two tons of it—at the cottage. My suspicions were aroused at first sight. Good coal usually looks bright and brittle; this stuff slid off the lorry in flat shaley-looking slabs that made almost a metallic noise. When I put some on the fire it lay there sluggishly, defying heat or flame to ignite it; the chimney blew down smoke, no doubt in protest at the filthy stuff going up it. It was easily the least combustible fuel I had ever seen. Somewhat exasperated I got on the 'phone to the undertaker. He was not at home, I was told, but a voice I had never heard before and most emphatically never wish to hear again asked me in rich Highland accents if it could be of any help.

'I wanted to know if there was a chance of getting hold

of some coal,' I said.

'More coal? Surely, Miss Peckwitt, you took two tons of coal last week just. What have you done with that?'

'I'm building a castle with it,' I retorted acridly. 'I want to talk about coal, not this rubbish.'

'Indeed, and isn't it terrible stuff? My own mother was saying herself just last night that she might as well carry dung from the byre and try will it burn.'

'Well, that's an idea anyway,' I conceded. 'I suppose if this was India we might be able to do that.'

'Do what? Use cow dung? For fuel, you say?'

'So I believe.'

'Indeed then, they must have very inflammable cows out there. I don't think it would work here at all. Supposing you tried mixing a little peat with the coal.'

'I have tried,' I said. 'It helps, certainly, but even so there's very little heat from it.'

'Ach, but you English,' the voice chided patiently, 'you're always complaining of feeling the cold.'

'It's no good sending me stones to keep me warm,' I retorted.

'No, indeed.' From the mouthpiece came the faintest of sighs. 'Well then, Miss Peckwitt,' the voice suggested blandly, 'will I come out myself tonight and have a damn good try?'

The months of April and May are regarded as being the best time for peat cutting so that the peats will have a chance to become thoroughly dry before the wet spell which can be relied upon to reach the Hebrides by the end of

June or early July. This year a faltering spring had delayed all the croft work and the hiccoughing cuckoos were already warning us that 'June was nearly away with the calendar' before a spell of fine weather was confidently predicted and Morag and I were able to set out together for the area of moor reserved for the village peat cutting. We followed first the track through the glen which, after years of agitation, the County Council had been persuaded to widen so that vans and lorries could reach some of the more isolated crofts where hitherto supplies had had to be carried by the women. Work on the project was slow and to all appearances involved the men in nothing more strenuous than chipping caves in rocky outcrops so as to provide shelter for them when at their card games.

'My, but you're busy,' Morag called as we passed a couple of them absorbed in scratching noughts and crosses on a face of rock.

'Aye.' They spared us a glance of tepid interest and then returned to their game.

'Indeed, I don't know why the County bothers to give them picks and shovels,' said Morag. 'I think it must be more for company than use.'

'They don't seem to do much work,' I agreed.

'Their main work is dodgin' the Gaffer. They wake him up in a mornin' to report for work and once they've done that then every time his back's turned they're out with their cards or else away up the hill with Donald's ferret. I canna' count the number of rabbits he's puttin' on the bus every mornin' since he's been working on the road.'

I glanced up towards the top of the hill and sure enough saw a straggling bunch of figures who looked as though they might be roadmen.

'You'd think,' I said, 'that they'd want to do some work occasionally, if only as a change from doing nothing.'

'That's just what Erchy told them now,' replied Morag warmly. 'Says he, "I'm sick of cards, cards, cards, I'm off to do some work," he says, and nobody stopped him!'

Bruach's peat glen was a sad, desolate-looking place, scarred by peat hags, some long neglected, and pocked with dark pools. The crofters, though they may not have cut peats for years, jealously guarded their rights to hags used by their forbears, their claims frequently encompassing quite large areas. Those who did rely on peat for fuel were continually forced to take out new hags further afield as the old ones became exhausted, and as a consequence it was usually the poorest and least accessible hags that were regularly worked while the best hags, close to the track for easy transport, were reserved for people who would never cut peat again, either because they were in the money or in their graves.

The only hag available for me was naturally one of the inaccessible ones. We turned off the track in its direction, the sodden moor squeaking protest at our every step. The previous day rain had fallen heavily and the hills, marble black against a paling blue sky, were still veined with white rushing burns whose muted thunder pressed at our ears. Now, the fresh-laundered sun was kindling the torches of asphodel into golden flame and coaxing the limp bog cotton to dry its plumage in the frisky breeze that sent contingents of ripples scurrying across the moorland pools.

' 'Tis a right day for the peats,' said Morag, 'but if this wind drops the clegs will eat us.'

'I wish there was a better path to my peats,' I said as we jumped dark drains and wallowed in spongy moss.

'Right enough,' replied Morag, 'but a few years ago you might have been glad of it.'

'How?' I asked.

'Indeed, but it's only a few years just since the scholars had each to take a peat with them to school every day for the fire and it's no the hags back here they'd be taking the peats from. No, it was always the easy ones nearest the road they took instead of their own. There was plenty of miscallings and skelpings about it in those days, but they never stopped them. My own bairns was as bad as the rest.'

My peats had already been 'stripped' for me by Erchy, which means that he had taken off the thick matted top layer of heather roots and turf, exposing the soft black peat. Stripping is traditionally a man's job and I was heartily glad it was so, for the widow Mary, who had given me the use of the hag, had confided that she believed its toughness had helped her husband into his grave. ('Ach, if you'd seen the man she had,' said Morag, who would have liked to cull the substandard of any species, when I told her; 'nothing but a long drink of gruel and his trousers near fallin' off the backside of him for want of somethin' to hold them up.') In Bruach, the fact that a job is heavy or strenuous did not necessarily mean that it was classed as a 'man's job'. It was, as I soon found out, mostly the women who did the heavy work of carrying and lifting, no matter what their age, shape or condition, and they seemed to pride themselves on their ability. The first time I saw an able-bodied crofter watching indifferently while his wife laboured under the burden of a boll of meal (140 lb.) I was provoked to the point of remonstrance. When, a few days later, I saw the same crofter meeting his dressed-up wife off the bus after a day's shopping on the mainland and chivalrously carrying her shopping basket, I was speechless. But gradually I grew to accept such things, so much so that I was only amused when I heard that Alistair Beag, a lazy man even by Bruach standards, had been taken to hospital after rupturing himself when trying to lift a load on to his wife's back. And then came a day when an old gallant, seeing me carrying home a sack of peat, said admiringly, 'My, my, but you have a good back for carrying,' and I was startled to find I had accepted it as a compliment.

Morag and I took turns at the cutting and throwing out of the peat, as we had done when I had shared her cottage and she was teaching me the essentials of a crofting life. I could of course have cut peats by myself, but it would have been a slow business. One cannot hurry peat cutting, but two people can establish a rhythm that more than halves the time and the work. I unashamedly enjoy working at the peats and not only because of a certain squirrel-like tendency which even in town was sometimes difficult to repress. It is satisfying to be mining for oneself; to be one's own coal merchant; to know that the harder one worked in the spring—always provided the weather played its part—the bigger fires one could indulge in when winter came. I see the glow of the fire in each peat as it is cut and tell myself: so many to keep my feet warm; so many to keep my back warm; now we have cut enough to burn for an hour; now for a day.

Peat cutting is one of the most companionable and one of the messiest jobs in the world. The cutter cuts; the soggy, chocolate-brown slices tilt into the waiting hands of the thrower out; there is a dull thud as the peat hits the heathery ground, releasing the scent of crushed bog-myrtle, or, if the aim is not particularly good, there is a resounding smack, succulent as a Louis Armstrong kiss, as it lands on its predecessor. The mud spreads up your arms—over your ankles; the sun beats on your back or your face depending on whether you cut or throw; the wind blows comfortable coolth. As you work, you and your companion discuss tranquilly the problems of your neighbours, of the country, of the world and, as the heather becomes progressively patterned with peat, you drift deeper into philosophy. So engrossed do you become that you do not notice that the wind has subsided briefly until the vicious clegs fasten on your bare limbs and you forget philosophy and filth and slap at the beastly things until you are a pattern of chocolate-brown yourself.

We stopped for lunch. In books on crofting life I have seen delightful photographs and descriptions of tablecloths being spread on the moor for the crofter families' alfresco meal while at the peats. I look upon them with the utmost scepticism. Perhaps it was the custom years ago; perhaps it was by arrangement with the photographer. Certainly, I have never seen it happen in Bruach, nor have I ever met anyone who recollected it happening. Why a crofter wife who normally sees no necessity to set a table for a meal in the house, let alone use a tablecloth, should make work for herself by taking a tablecloth to spread on the moor when such a dirty job as peat cutting is involved I cannot understand. Morag and I pulled bundles of moss and wiped our hands to a uniform brown and ate oatcakes and crowdie and peat. We cupped our hands and drank water from the well where a family of robbers were said to have disposed of the bodies of their victims. It was very good water. And then we started cutting again. A normal supply of peats for a household not using coal is nine good stacks, which means some thousands of peats. We reckoned we cut at the rate of about ten a minute—six hundred an hour—and we carried on until the breeze dropped away completely, the sun was threatening to dehydrate us and we could no longer stand the onslaught of the clegs.

'I'm badly needin' a cup of tea,' said Morag. We straightened our backs, shouldered our tools and retraced our path to the road.

Work on the road had made no noticeable progress during the day. Some of the men, under the eye of the now alert Gaffer, were chipping languidly at the rock while others were loading the chippings into a lorry with a deliberation which suggested that they were rationing the number of pieces on their shovels before attempting to raise them from the ground.

'Hear the Gaffer gettin' right mad with them,' said Morag with evident relish, 'and isn't my fine fellows enjoyin' themselves. Tormentin' him till they have him hoppin' about like a hen on a hot girdle.'

The Gaffer was an ex-seaman and his vocabulary when provoked was reputed to make the hills blush. We coughed and talked louder than was necessary as we approached and the abruptness with which his stream of abuse ceased was equalled by the alacrity with which the men ceased their work. He was a short, leathery old man who walked about with his hands tucked into his waistcoat and with the air of someone looking for a place to spit. It was rumoured in Bruach that he was a secret admirer of Morag's and as he turned to greet us his thick lips were stretched in a fatuous smile.

'Wass you at the peats?' he asked superfluously.

'We was till this minute,' replied Morag. 'But the clegs was murderin' us once the wind dropped and we could stand it no longer.'

'Aye, right enough,' agreed the Gaffer, 'they'd be bad at the peats. And yet can you believe it they can come all round me and I've never been bitten yet. It's funny that now, isn't it?'

'It's no funny at all,' interpolated the driver of the lorry. 'Clegs is teetotal. One sup of your blood and they'd die of alcoholic poisoning.'

The Gaffer's capacity for drink was phenomenal and always a source of awed comment and speculation in Bruach.

It was said that when he had been ill the previous year the hospital had found it necessary to allocate to him a special blood group—White Horse. It was said that the doctors had found it necessary to wear gas masks when taking a blood sample for fear they would get drunk on the fumes. But, despite his addiction, it was rare for the Gaffer to make an exhibition of himself. He imbibed in the seclusion of his hut and only the men who, with true Gaelic warm-heartedness, hovered around to see he did himself no harm, witnessed and reported the state he drank himself into. The only time I was aware of his being even moderately inebriated was when I had been a passenger on the bus one evening and we had got stuck in a snowdrift. Spades were invariably carried in the back of the bus for just such a contingency and the male passengers each took one and set to work to dig us out. All day a blizzard had been blowing but now, though the wind had dropped, the snow was still falling with steady menace. It was bitterly cold and the men were too wrapped up mentally and physically to notice the Gaffer, whose reaction to having a spade thrust into his hands was to shovel and lift, shovel and lift. This he did, loading snow enthusiastically into the mails compartment of the bus through the open rear door and inappropriately accompanying his exertions with a quaintly original version of 'Fire Down Below' which he rendered with trumpet-tongued disharmony.

The Gaffer's smile broadened reluctantly as the men chuckled over the driver's badinage.

'Gaffer, go and brew up a cup of tea for the ladies, they'll be needin' one,' Erchy suggested gallantly. 'And I believe I'll take a cup myself while you're at it.'

'Tea!' The word burst from the Gaffer's throat like a gas jet extinguishing itself with its own ferocity.

'Aye, tea,' the voice repeated. 'Aren't you always tellin' us what a great one you used to be for entertainin' the ladies? Well then, see and go and brew up a cup of tea for them now while you've the chance. An' don't forget us lot. We're damty dry with all the work we're after doin', aren't we, boys?'

The Gaffer looked as though he was about to spit but catching Morag's eye he swallowed and admitted cautiously: 'The kettle's boilin' for my own tea. Will you take a cup if I made it?'

'In my hand,' consented Morag, whom I had never known refuse a cup of tea no matter what the situation or circumstance.

He disappeared inside his hut as with startled winks and delighted chortles the men opened up their haversacks and produced a variety of sturdy mugs which they set out on an upturned wheelbarrow. We all made ourselves comfortable on boulders and on other upturned wheelbarrows. Cigarettes were handed round; pipes were lit. After a few minutes the truckling Gaffer reappeared carrying a steaming kettle and a tin of condensed milk; at the sight of his audacious henchmen placidly enjoying the interlude a certain lugubriousness was restored to his features but again he swallowed and forbore to comment.

'Careful with that stuff, Gaffer,' quipped one of the men

as he proceeded to pour out black tea from the kettle. 'It's that strong I'm thinkin' it will be crackin' the cups.' As I accepted a cup my stomach quailed at the thought of drinking it. Under the pretext of waiting for it to cool I lazily transposed the mosaic of gravel caught in a cleft of rock beside me and watched everyone else alternately gulping tea and extracting suicidal clegs from sticky cups. The pleasantries between Gaffer and men continued unceasingly, and I was able to take advantage of a particularly amusing volley to tilt my cup surreptitiously into a convenient hillock of moss.

'It's queer to me,' said Morag, as she finished her tea and stood up, 'why you folks don't use gelatine for blowin' up all this rock, save havin' to chip at it day after day like you're after doin'.'

'My God,' breathed the Gaffer piously, 'I'd have no head left to think with and no legs left to run away with if you put gelignite in reach of these buggers. Why, that man, there,' the Gaffer went on, pointing an accusing finger at Neilac, 'he came near to killin' me with his pick yesterday, never mind gelignite.'

'It was an accident,' retorted Neilac complacently; 'and anyway, what's it matter if I did kill you; you'd still keep wrigglin' like an eel, there's that much of the Devil in you.'

'If you killed me first and then stripped the skin off me, my bones would keep on movin',' retorted the Gaffer, who seemed to accept that his body was just a collection of bones laced together with whisky.

Murdoch, an indomitable old man who could always

be found where there was money to be made no matter how trivial or how hazardous the effort involved, was perched on a section of up-ended culvert pipe looking at his watch which he took from a tin in his pocket.

'Yes, what is the time?' Morag asked him.

'Wait and I'll tell you,' muttered Murdoch, still studying his watch.

'How that man knows the time with a watch that has the minute hand so short you can't tell it from the hour hand I don't know,' said the Gaffer.

'Indeed, if I watch it long enough I can see one of them move,' replied Murdoch.

'That's not what you're here for,' expostulated the Gaffer, jumping up and giving Murdoch a push in the chest that sent the old man buttocks down into the culvert pipe. 'Get that lorry finished loadin'.'

'Here, here, man,' remonstrated Murdoch indignantly, 'I canna' load a lorry with my arse tight in a drainpipe. Have sense, man.'

Laughingly the men pulled Murdoch out of his predicament and sauntered back to their work.

' 'Tis five o'clock then,' announced Murdoch as he returned his watch to his pocket.

The men froze animatedly and awaited the Gaffer's corroboration.

' 'Tis no more than five to,' he said firmly. 'Get on with it.' Watch in hand, he urged them on to fill the lorry and as the minute finger touched the hour he took a whistle from his pocket and blew. The men with picks arrested their strokes mid-way; the men loading tilted their shovels so that the chippings slid back on to the road and then they threw down their implements, collected their jackets and bags and hoisted themselves on to the lorry.

'Look at that,' called the Gaffer caustically. 'In a big enough hurry to knock off at night they are, but never one of them here on time this mornin'.'

'That's a lie!' Tom-Tom, an excitable muddle-headed little man, squeaked in protest.

'That's as true as I'm here,' asseverated the Gaffer.

'It's a lie, I'm tellin' you,' spluttered Tom-Tom, jumping down from the lorry and confronting the Gaffer with all his five foot nothing of bristling indignation. 'I was here in good time. I know because I jumped straight out of my bed when I heard the wireless time and indeed I came out in such a rush I left the door in bed and my wife wide open.'

The faces of the men remained impassive and the Gaffer checked a wheeze of laughter before setting his face into a scowl which he bestowed upon the driver who, with one hand in his pocket, was trying nonchalantly to crank his lorry.

'What like of a man is that?' asked the Gaffer contemptuously. 'Tryin' will he start a lorry with one of his hands stuck in his pocket.'

The driver put both hands into his pockets and regarded the Gaffer coolly.

'Who's grumblin' about my hands bein' in my pockets?'

'I am,' exploded the Gaffer.

'Well, at least my hand's in my own pocket,' retaliated

the driver, the grin plucking at his lips belying the testiness of his voice. 'You keep your grumblin' till you find them in your own pockets.' He stepped up into the cab and gave a long pull on the self-starter which coaxed the engine into a clatter of activity. The men lifted their hands in farewell gestures that ranged from the sickly to the regal as the lorry jogged away round the bend.

'Look at them,' commented Morag acidly; 'wouldn't you think it was to a convalescent home the lorry was takin' them.'

III. *Just Hector*

'Tsere is a tsing,' said Hector appealingly. 'A tsing in tse shed at tse back of tse house, will mend it. Callum said I would get it if I wanted it.'

I took a deep breath and the key of the shed from the drawer and accompanied Hector to ferret out his 'tsing'.

Within a few months of having bought the cottage from Callum I was getting thoroughly tired of having his name quoted in exoneration of their actions by those who descended upon me with predatory intent. Callum, it transpired, had hurriedly disposed of everything movable in and around the cottage as soon as I had popped up as a prospective buyer. There had been a useful store of peat in one of the sheds which I had thought would help me through the winter but a week or so after I had settled in when, I suppose, the unmistakable blue of peat smoke had been seen eddying from my chimney, visitors had come in the night with sacks and appropriated the lot. Had I been a Gael I should either have nursed my grievance until there was a chance to retaliate or I should have referred to it obliquely, perhaps blaming the fairies. I did neither.

'Why did you come in the night and take peats from my shed?' I taxed the offenders.

'Indeed they were no your peats at all,' they retorted loftily. 'Callum said we could have them a while ago, but we left them till we would get a chance to move them.'

'Then why couldn't you have told me and taken them in the daylight instead of coming at night?'

'Why? Did we frighten you? Ach, we're awful sorry. If we'd known you were going to be frightened we would have come some other time right enough. We just thought we wouldn't disturb you.'

Similar appropriations happened every other month or so to begin with. A pair of wheels and an axle which I had annexed for making into some sort of a box cart were claimed immediately I made known my intention and I had to endure being thanked effusively for having looked after them so long. A boat-hook and a pair of oars were spirited away when it was discovered I was looking around for a dinghy; a sack of fleece which I had envisaged having spun into knitting wool likewise vanished. Always the excuse was 'Callum said. . . .' I padlocked the shed eventually and though admittedly the claims decreased they have not ceased altogether during the years, and I am still apprehensive that the massive lump of oak which was once an engine bearer in a boat and is now my mantelpiece will some day be recognized and desired by someone with an irrefutable claim to it, or that I shall wake up one morning to find the cattle breakfasting in my garden because the shafts of a cart which make the gate to keep them out have been requisitioned for their original purpose.

By far the most persistent claimant was Morag's nephew, Hector, who had now returned to Bruach with his wife and child to settle on his aunt's croft. Before his return Hector had been rather a shadowy character, rarely alluded to by Morag or anyone else until he had met with the accident, the alleged effects of which were bringing him back to Bruach. Once it was known he was coming his name was soon on everyone's lips. His transgressions were remembered and related with glee. Hector was the son of Morag's sister who, according to Morag, had married a real bad man, English of course, who had soon left her to bring up their son as best she could. She had brought the boy to the home of her parents and there let him run wild. Morag strongly disapproved of Hector's upbringing.

'My sister didn't believe in skelpin',' she lamented to me. 'She used to say you can't knock sense into a lad's head by thrashin' his backside, but I was always after tellin' her that sense can work its way up from the bottom to the top same as everythin' else in this world.'

It seemed however that Hector had not entirely escaped thrashing.

'Always takin' the day off from school to go fishin' he was,' Erchy told me. 'One mornin' he went fishin' off the

Black rock and he fell into the sea. He was near drowned but for Big Willie bein' out in his boat and pickin' him up in time. He was brought into school. Ach, we thought he was dead right enough, but the teacher turned him over and squeezed a lot of water out of him. By God! The teacher was that mad with him as soon as he came to he lay him across the desk and thrashed him till his pants steamed. That cured Hector of drownin' and of playin' truant from school, I can tell you.'

Hector's main claim to notoriety though, as everyone admitted, was his success with women.

'Hell, what a man he was,' Erchy told me reverently. 'Used to carve his initials on every rock he'd taken a women behind, and when we go after the deer in the hills we keep comin' across these "H.M.S.s" chipped all over the place. Makes you feel hot to see them there's that many. Honest, he's as bad as the stags themselves, that man.'

'Perhaps marriage has changed him,' ventured someone, but from the way the suggestion was received it was obvious that no one really believed Hector could change appreciably.

I naturally expected to meet an Adonis, but when Morag brought him to my cottage I was confronted by a middle-aged man, with thinning black hair and with a pale, marrow-shaped face, carelessly shaven and deeply lined between nose and mouth. He was tall and well made but he drooped despondently over his stomach and jumbled his arms and legs about when he walked. He had, however, a pair of very beguiling blue eyes, a charmingly shy smile and a unique gift for making every woman he paid even the scantest attention to feel that she was someone very, very special. He exerted a little of his charm on me that day and I succumbed immediately, despite all the warnings I had been given. I was soon deluding myself that never again should I have to wait for someone to do for me the little jobs that were beyond my capabilities; that Hector's strong arm would always be ready with help whenever I needed it; that I should always be a welcome guest aboard his boat; that a fish would be procured for me, one way or another, whenever I might express a fancy for one. For hours after he had gone I glowed with satisfaction.

The very next day Hector came and enlisted my help to haul up his boat for repairs. *Wayfarer* was a thirty-two foot motor-boat, heavily built and deeply keeled, and I felt rather as though I were taking part in an ill-matched tug-o'-war when I was harnessed, along with most of the able-bodies in the village, male and female, to a thick rope and exhorted repeatedly to heave. We strained and sweated, our feet shifting and skidding on the shingle, while all the time Hector, who had to keep an eye on a 'tsing', appeared to do nothing more strenuous than caress the boat's stern.

A few days after the boat hauling I started clearing out my sheds and Hector, who had proffered help, stepped in only to assert his claim whenever I discovered anything useful and to magnanimously bestow on me anything that was not. I soon found that most of what I thought I had paid for had been previously disposed of to him by Callum— even an old log basket which had been woven for me by a friend, but which he confidently asserted was one of his grandfather's unorthodox creels. I found too that while he was not averse to sitting in the kitchen drinking innumerable cups of tea, his capacity for which was even more impressive than his Aunt's, he melted away like the mist when I gave the slightest hint that I should like some help. He would sometimes go fishing if I agreed to row him about while he dangled a line, but it was in Hector's company that I was able to prove that the old fisherman's belief, 'If a red-haired woman crosses your path when you are going out fishing you may as well go home because you will not catch a fish', is no idle superstition. A red-haired woman once crossed our path and Hector promptly abandoned me and any ideas of fishing and took off in pursuit.

There were undoubtedly times when Hector's behaviour was infuriating, yet I could no more have vented my spleen on him than I could have thrown a stone at a blackbird stealing the strawberries in my garden. He was weak, but he was lovable, gentle, philosophical, and so kind-hearted that the word 'no' simply did not come into his vocabulary. Sooner than make someone momentarily unhappy by a refusal he would promise faithfully anything at all, without having the slightest intention of keeping his promise. If anyone reproached him he assumed an utterly dejected air, his blue eyes would open wide and he would start to explain haltingly how some 'tsing' had prevented him from keeping his word.

Hector could be in turn gallantly attentive, shy and gangling and guilelessly candid. In a moment of confidence

one day he whipped up his shirt and showed me the operation scar on his stomach and seemed disappointed when I
did not whip up my skirts and show him mine. Though he
came to regard my cottage much as a second home and to
feel that he knew me too well to address me as 'Miss
Peckwitt', he could never permit himself the familiarity of
using my name (Gaelicized as 'Lilac') or the diminutive
'Becky' by which I am known to my friends. In conversation he referred to me as 'she' with a nod in the direction
of my cottage or my presence. If he wished to attract my
attention for any reason, he would sidle up to me and give
me a companionable slap on the behind. This aversion to
using my Christian name persisted even when he adopted
the disturbing habit of kissing me good-bye. He would lum-
ber across the kitchen towards me, fling his arms around
me and, because I dodged expertly, land a kiss somewhere
on the back of my neck. It was the utterly simple, warm-
hearted kiss of a child, or of a brother or sister, grateful for
understanding. At first I had wondered if I should permit it
but it was gradually borne in upon me that every time he
kissed me good-bye some tool or other useful article disappeared from the cottage on loan. Once it was my nail
brush and when it was surreptitiously returned I realized
from the smell in the bathroom that it had been used for
scrubbing the 'berries' off 'berried' lobsters which are not
allowed by law to be marketed. Once it was my toothbrush
which came back reeking of oil and petrol, no doubt after
having been used to clean a 'tsing' in his engine. Another
time it was my paraffin drum because his own had devel-

oped a leak. Dusters he collected and stowed away in his boat much as a park attendant collects waste paper and I grew accustomed to seeing my cast-off under and outer clothing wrapping greasy tools or used for swabbing down decks. Though eventually I came to accept this good-bye kiss as pure camouflage, at first there were times when I rebelled at his perfidy and avoided his embrace. Then he would slouch away and not return for several days or even weeks. The last time I had practised such an evasion Behag, Hector's wife, had come to see me the next day. Behag was a fat, pallid voiced, sagging little woman whose only interests in life seemed to be her child, her retinue of cats and the knitting of colourful pullovers for her husband. She was curiously placid and remained completely indifferent to her husband's affairs unless they were right under her nose and even then she evinced only tolerant amusement. I liked her tremendously and thought she deserved so much better than she had got but she was content with the way things were. As she got up to go, which is the time all Gaels reserve for the offhand disclosure of the real reason for their visit, she had asked anxiously: 'Were you cross with Hector last night, Miss Peckwitt?'

'Yes, a little,' I had admitted briefly.

'And last Thursday week, no it wasn't Thursday but Friday. You were cross with him then too, were you not?'

'Perhaps. I can't remember.'

'I can,' she had said sorrowfully. 'I can always tell.'

'Can you? But how?' I had asked.

'Because if you won't let him kiss you good-bye, he

comes home and he kicks the cats,' she had told me with infinite pathos.

Today, Hector wanted a 'tsing' for his engine. It was time his boat was launched for the summer tourist trade, he said, and though he had scraped and 'bottomed' her and patched any leaks with tingles he was now having trouble with the engine. My shed was by now reasonably tidy. If only Hector had shifted the boxes of ancient engine parts he so much cherished I might have been able to whitewash it and fit it out for its eventual use as a dairy. He tipped up one of the boxes, cascaded wheels, nuts, washers and unidentifiable lumps of rust on to the floor and scrabbled through them. I watched him unhelpfully.

'I wonder at you, Hector,' I said. 'You've had such a lot of work to do on this boat and yet you told me you spent quite a long time looking for a good one when you were in Glasgow.'

Hector sat back on his heels and clasped his chin with rusty fingers. 'Well, you know how it is,' he explained slowly. 'You go lookin' for a boat like you go lookin' for a wife. You wander from place to place having a good look first at one and tsen at another. If you find exactly what you want and tse price is right, tsen you say, "Ach, she's too cheap, tsere must be somsing wrong with her," and like as not you end up with gettin' tse worst.' He bent again over the scatter of things on the floor and extracted an object which seemed to give him some satisfaction.

'I'll just try will tsis do,' he said. 'I'll need to come back and clear up tsese tsings for you.'

That was the last I saw of him for about a week.

When he came again I was at the far end of the croft from the house, trying my skill at building up a collapsed drystone wall. Hector must have seen me but he sprackled across the croft with the deceptive aimlessness of a hen on her way to a secret nest.

'You're busy,' he greeted me.

'Yes. Are you any good at building up walls, Hector?'

'No indeed, I was never any good at it, tsough I remember my grandfather always used to say to keep my middle well filled.' He teetered one or two of the stones I thought I had wedged in position but he was too polite to comment.

'She looks as tsough she'll make a nice day yet,' he murmured.

'You think so?'

'Aye. Too nice for a funeral, anyway.'

'Whose funeral?'

'Well, you see, an uncle of Behag's has died and he's bein' buried today and Behag tsinks I should go. What do you tsink yourself?'

'If Behag thinks you should go she's probably right,' I replied. 'But how will you get there if the funeral's today? The bus has gone long ago.'

'Well,' he admitted, 'tsat's tse way of it.'

I realized that I was going to have to insist on taking him in 'Joanna'.

'Ach, it's no right. I'm givin' you too much trouble,' he said as I expected him to.

'Not at all,' I replied, as he expected me to. 'How soon do you want to go?'

'I was wonderin'. You see I have a box of mackerel I got tsis mornin' just and I tsought maybe if we could put it in tse back I could sell it to one or two of tse hotels on tse way. If we could start out early enough, say in about an hour's time.'

I left my stone-building and went to get myself and 'Joanna' ready, not really sorry to be taken away from my work for a day out even if it were for a funeral. The service was to take place at the hospital where the old man had died and I should not be expected to attend it. It was just a matter of taking Hector up, collecting him after an hour or so and then bringing him back. At least, that is what I thought in my innocence.

All dressed up in his best blue suit and cap, Hector was waiting by the gate of Morag's cottage when I stopped 'Joanna'. He lifted the box of fish into the boot and came and got in beside me. Morag and Behag, colourful figures in the silvery morning sunshine, waved to us from their work on the croft.

'Tse cailleach tsinks it's goin' to rain,' said Hector as he settled himself. 'She's wantin' to get all the tatties cleaned before she comes.' I wondered fleetingly if it really was at Behag's insistence that Hector was dashing away to her uncle's funeral.

Our run was extremely pleasant. The sun spent long periods in moody retirement but the rain disported itself only across the outlying islands, and left us alone. Hector pointed out a hotel and asked me to drive round to the back door. He disappeared inside and ten minutes later came out again followed by two very capable-looking ladies, one carrying a white pail and a cloth. They went round to the boot, some discussion went on and they all three went back into the hotel. I stayed in 'Joanna'. Hector soon came out, wiping the back of his hand across his mouth, and rejoined me and we drove on to another hotel where much the same thing happened. Hector finally emerged, once more wiping his mouth and growing noticeably more benign. At the third hotel, once the transaction was over, I was invited by the housekeeper into the kitchen for a cup of tea, an invitation which by this time I was very glad to accept. The kitchen of the hotel was large and cool and refreshingly clean. A long white wood table, scoured to perfection, ran down the centre; at one end was a tempting-looking tea-tray laid for two and at the opposite end there was a scale and a large dish of silvery trout. The grateful smile and the words of thanks I was uttering died away as I stared first at the trout and then at Hector.

'Hector!' I ejaculated hoarsely. But Hector sat with his knees locked girlishly together, rubbing the palms of his hands slowly up and down his thighs, and except for a couple of furtive glances in my direction, concentrated his attention on the decorative fly-catcher which hung from the ceiling. I was appalled. Here I had been driving round with a box of illicit fish in the boot of my car and everyone who had seen me and the friends and relations of everyone who had seen me would be quite certain that I was in this poach-

ing business up to my neck. I was so shocked at his treach-
ery that I drank little and ate less of the 'strupak' that was
offered me and even that gave me indigestion.

'Hector,' I upbraided when we were outside again, 'I
can't forgive you for this. You've really gone too far.'

'Ach, but nobody worries about a bit of poachin' nowadays,' he soothed. 'So long as it's not too much. And someone else would have tsem if I didn't take tsem myself.'

'You could have been honest with me,' I said 'You could
have told me they were trout, not mackerel.'

'Ach, well now, surely you'd know tse hotels wouldn't
want to be buyin' mackerel from me?'

'Are there any more left?' I demanded, abashed at my
own stupidity.

'Just about four, maybe the half dozen. Ach, we'll not
worry about tsem. You can take tsem for your dinner.'

'You know perfectly well I wouldn't dream of taking
them, but I do want them out of my car,' I told him.

'Aye, tsen, I'll take tsem in a wee minute, but see and
just come with me to the shop now before tsey close. I'd
like you to help me choose a tsing for Behag,' he wheedled.

I yielded sufficiently to choose a lovely fair-isle jersey
for Behag and to help him buy some sweets for Fiona and
Morag. We were on our way back to the car when Hector
muttered suddenly: 'Oh, my God.'

'What is it?' I asked. He was staring across the road at
a policeman who was standing near the kerb. My knees
started to feel a little weak. I recalled hearing of poaching
penalties which included the confiscation of the offender's car.

'He'll see me in a minute,' muttered Hector. 'Here, take tsese.' He thrust the parcels at me.

'What's the matter?' I asked agitatedly.

'He'll want to shake hands with me,' Hector replied. 'I used to know him well and I haven't seen him for years,' and then added by way of explanation, 'I should have asked to wash my hands at that hotel, tsese bloody trout scales stick like glue. Are tsere any on my cuffs?' He displayed his right hand liberally dotted with unmistakeable trout scales and then rubbed it vigorously on the seat of his trousers. We were approaching the policeman who, turning, caught sight of Hector. His face split into a grin as he came across the road to greet him. Hector's hand rubbed even more vigorously behind him. 'God!' I heard him mutter desperately.

The policeman put out his hand, grasped Hector's and shook it firmly. As soon as it was released Hector plunged both hands deep into his jacket pockets and kept them there.

'Tsat's a nice fellow,' he told me when everything had passed off serenely, 'but all tse same, if I'd known he was in tsis part of tse world I wouldn't have wanted him to see me.' I made no comment. 'I'd best go to tse service now,' he said when we were putting the parcels in the car and after I had discovered that it was early-closing day so that my shopping would not get done.

'You'll get rid of those trout before you do anything else, Hector,' I insisted firmly.

'Oh yes, aye, aye.' He heaved a big sigh. 'I wonder what will I do with tsem?'

'I was expecting you to say you'd present them to the

policeman,' I said with bitter sarcasm.

Hector looked at me with surprised approval. 'I could do tsat too,' he rejoined. 'I'll see will I get a wee bitty paper to wrap tsem in.'

'Hector,' I called despairingly, but he was hurrying away. I cringed behind the wheel of 'Joanna' and shut my eyes as he bowled confidently through the open door of the police station opposite. I opened them again when I heard him at the boot. He came round to the door of the car with a box tucked under his arm.

'I won't be more tsan a minute,' he assured me happily. I could not bring myself to ask him what had happened, but before very long he was back at the car again, whistling discordantly. 'I'm away to tse service now,' he said.

'What did you do with the trout?' I managed to ask weakly.

'Ach well, I went into tse pollis station and asked for him but tsey said he was takin' his dinner, so I went round to see his wife, and told her I wanted a wee bitty paper or a box to put somesing tasty in for her man's dinner. She gave me a box and so tsat's got rid of tsat lot.' He sighed. 'Well, I'd best be away,' he repeated, but he had reckoned without the grateful attention of the policeman who now came hurrying towards the car. Hector beamed complacently as once again his hand was grasped and shaken. But this time it was the policeman's hands that were covered in fish scales.

When Hector returned from the service he asked me if I would mind very much following the hearse back to the burial ground instead of returning straight to Bruach, as we had originally intended. Behag's uncle, he explained, had been something of a reprobate and had cut himself off from the family. As a consequence Hector had been the only mourner and he thought Behag would not like it if he left the old man to go alone to his final resting place. Though I suspected in this arrangement a design to await the evening opening of the pubs before returning home I fell in with it because it meant that I should be able to see part of the Island I had never seen before. While Hector supervised the actual interment, I thought, I could wander over the moors looking for wild flowers of which there might be some species not found in Bruach.

When we arrived at the burial ground we were met by a trio of indignant grave diggers who roused themselves from their perches on listing tombstones to inform us that they had not received a word about preparing a grave until an hour ago. They had the cows to milk and other chores to do tonight and they couldn't get the grave finished until morning.

'What'll we do with him for tse night tsen?' asked Hector.

'We could put him in the church,' suggested one of the trio. The grave diggers and the driver of the hearse carried the coffin into the church. Hector watched them impassively.

'You know,' he said when we were seated again in 'Joanna' and heading for Bruach, 'I tsink tsat's likely tse first time tse old man has ever been in church in his life.'

I dropped Hector at Morag's cottage and because I was still feeling aggrieved over the business of the trout I made an excuse not to go in for a 'strupak'. I supposed both Morag and Behag knew that it was a box of poached trout Hector had loaded into my car that morning but as no Bruachite really believes poaching in moderation to be a crime they would have assumed that I also knew and approved.

I had barely finished feeding my poultry and having my own tea when Hector sparked in through the gate in a new electric blue and viridian pullover. He came with a saucer of fresh-made butter from Morag and really sincere offers to help me with one or two jobs which he knew perfectly well I had already done for myself. He sat on the bench watching me as I cleared the table and washed the dishes, too ashamed and embarrassed to keep up a conversation but humming every now and then to show me how much at ease he felt. I had some letters to write and I wished he would go but I could not bring myself to say 'I mustn't keep you back', which is the accepted Gaelic way of telling anyone 'For goodness's sake, go!' My expression must have been a little forbidding because he tried several times to draw a smile from me by telling me feeble jokes. At last he could bear it no longer.

'I wish I hadn't made you cross with tse fish,' he said miserably.

'Oh, I suppose it's all right,' I conceded stiffly.

He got up and lumbered towards me, his arms outstretched. I remembered the cats, and capitulated.

IV. *Beachcombing*

ONE OF THE CHIEF DELIGHTS of living in Bruach was that there was always an excuse to go rambling along the seashore in search of driftwood for kindling. To negotiate much of the tide line one needed to be fairly agile. It was a matter of leaping from one slippery rock to another whilst wearing equally slippery gumboots; of wallowing ankle-deep in sodden tangle; of wading through shell-strewn pools, and sometimes climbing up steep barnacle-encrusted rocks to skirt the incoming tide. To me it was all sheer glory. With the sharp clean smell of the sea filling my nostrils, the roaring of the breakers in my ears and the astringent caress of fine spray on my cheeks I was content to wander for hours. The dominant motive was always to gather driftwood, but it was difficult to resist the fascination of collecting a few limpets or winkles to smash and feed to the waving tendrils of the anemones in the colourful pools, or turning over a stone to watch the green crabs scuttling to fresh hiding places. There was always plenty of driftwood and one began by collecting every piece and making little piles along the shore to be collected on the return journey, but always, a little farther along, there were choicer pieces of driftwood than those one had already gathered and so one continued acquisitively until there were far too many piles to be carried home and one had to select the most desirable pieces and leave the rest, hoping it would be there another day.

Apart from driftwood, the assortment of objects washed ashore was limitless. Tins of American shaving cream (which Morag reckoned was splendid for washing Hector's sweaty socks); plastic cups; letters in bottles (very unromantic ones); oars; brooms; deck shoes; cans of paint. It was doubtless due to the finding of half-full tins of paint that the walls of my cottage had been such a peculiar colour. Once I found an undamaged vacuum flask which I use to this day. Once a necklace, and once, very fortuitously, a full tin of dripping. My bread-board is the door of a ship's locker; my door-stopper is the vertebra of a whale which visiting small dogs frequently linger to gnaw and visiting large dogs determinedly try to appropriate. My most treasured find to date is merely a piece of driftwood, part of the branch of a tree, but beautifully sculptured by nature into a classic representation of a female figure.

Many of my neighbours were dedicated beachcombers, sometimes spending stormy nights in convenient caves so as to be the first to pounce on any trophy the sea might bestow—no doubt kept warm by the unflagging hope that it might be a cask of whisky. I can recall someone finding a sack of flour which he claimed as quite fit for use because the flour on the outside formed into a paste which had kept the inside dry. Another found a box of candles which were certainly useful. From washed-up crates I have been given onions that were so impregnated with salt they needed none in the cooking, and grapefruit that were uneatable for the same reason. Such things as bales of rubber were at one time considered lucrative finds because in addition to the pound or two reward from the Receiver of Wrecks quite high freight charges could be claimed for rowing them to a convenient spot for collection. So long as these charges were paid undemurringly the Bruachites continued to increase them until they reaped the reward of their own avarice, the authorities deciding that the recovery of the rubber was no longer economical. So the bales were left to rot on the shore along with the pit props, trawl bobbins, net floats, old co-conut husks and fish baskets, which are the inevitable adorn-ments of the tangle-woven shingle.

In the autumn, after the hay and corn had been stacked for the winter and all the peats had been carried home from the moor, the Bruachites would go winkle picking for the Billingsgate market. Often when beachcombing I met groups of them working their way along the shore, filling pails with the shiny blue-black shells; carrying the full pails to tip into the waiting sacks, and carrying the full sacks up the brae to the lorry. There was supposed to be good money in winkle picking and as my budget was a tight one I thought I would like to try my hand at it. Wearing about three pullovers and with scarves round my middle, round my neck and over my head, and oilskins topping everything, I took my pail and followed the outgoing tide. Crouching low, my back towards the sea, I turned over rocks, seeing the sparks fly and smelling the sulphurous smell as they crashed against one another and exposed the writhing cat-fish, the spotted gunnels, the myriads of sandlice and the pathetically few winkles beneath them. Working my way up again, with the incoming tide chasing me inexorably, I discovered colonies of winkles, but before I could get more than a couple of handfuls of them into my pail the tide was swirling around my boots and over the winkles so that I could no longer see them to pick. A good picker can pick a bag or more in a single tide, that is two hours before and two hours after low tide. After a few days' practise I found I could manage about a pailful and there are five pailfuls to the sack. To get even that sad quantity I had to concentrate so much that when I shut my eyes at night I saw only troves of black glistening winkles and in my dreams reached out to gather them. I did, much to the astonishment of the other pickers, achieve a full sack eventually, but only by waiting another ten days or so for the next daylight low tide. In due course I received a cheque from a Billingsgate firm but the amount, after payment of the crippling freight charged by the railway, was no reward for my worn nails and sore chapped hands and the ache in my back caused by wrestling with stubborn boulders. Yet the Bruachites looked forward eagerly to the beginning of the winkling season and I came to understand their eagerness. The work could be squeezed in between the other chores and the money earned was always welcome. For some of the younger folk who could not go to the mainland for employment because of having to look after the old folks it was often their only chance to make some pocket money. They winkled, as they did so many things, in happy, chattering groups, never wandering out of earshot of one another; but though the sea stays comparatively warm until after the New Year, to crouch down for four long hours on an exposed shore, drenched with spray and with a bitterly cold wind hurling its icy daggers between your shoulder blades is a desperate way of earning money. Particularly when you have not even the comfort of a hot bath to look forward to but only a couple of kettles of hot water—if you first go to the well and fill a pail.

The most inveterate beachcomber and by far the speediest winkle picker in the village was 'Euan, the son of Euan, the son of Euan', the Gaelic pronunciation of whose name approximated to a long drawn-out yawn. He was a bright-eyed old man, always picturesquely dressed in an old peaked cap and a seaman's jersey—relics of his days on a yacht as a steward—and his legs bound round from the top of his tackety boots to above the knee with thick rope so that they resembled the legs of the Michelin Tyre man. He flatly refused to have anything to do with gumboots, saying that they 'cooked his feets', and stoutly maintaining that his strong hill-boots and rope puttees were more effective in keeping out the wet because it did not get a chance to leak over the top. Yawn had made some of the most envied finds on the shore. It was rumoured that he really had found a large cask of whisky and that he had secreted it somewhere in the hills.

'He's never without a dram in the house,' Postie assured everyone earnestly. 'And his pension doesn't give that to him.' As everyone was sure that Postie was bound to know exactly what Yawn's pension gave him they accepted the story of the secret cask and whenever Bruachites did not know what to do with themselves, as on Sunday afternoons, they were inclined to form into little bands of searchers for Yawn's treasure. As they always came back sober they obviously never found it.

Yawn lived with his two sisters on the croft next but one to my own. Brother and sisters were all over seventy and of the three only Yawn himself could read or write or tell the time. His two sisters were utterly unlike. Sarah, the younger one (seventy-four), was a delightfully bobbish little lady doing all the housework and most of the croft work with never a word of complaint except that she was tormented by her corns. The elder sister, Flora, had once been a lady's maid and could not bear to forget it. She sat stiffly all day long in a chair, commenting disparagingly on everything Sarah did and doing absolutely nothing else. She could neither read nor write. She did not knit, sew or darn. She would not move from her chair to cook or even to lift a boiling kettle from the fire. What little food she ate she took on a plate on her lap. She was not ill, nor paralysed in any way, but she had sat so still for so long that the chair seemed to have merged itself into her body and her body into the musty black skirts that clung to the floor as raggedly as old wainscoting so that one would not have been at all surprised to see mice darting in and out of them. On her head she wore the most impressive tea cosy of hair it is possible to imagine. It completely overbalanced her face and marvelling at the edifice I sometimes wondered if the weight of it was responsible for the apparent fixation of her body and mind. It was said in Bruach, and I can well believe it, that she had not touched her hair with comb or brush, soap or water, for over forty years; that if it was investigated thoroughly the remains of at least half a dozen hair nets and several hundred hairpins would be discovered, all completely enjungled. Some recalled with awe that before her hair grew quite so matted she had been seen to reach for the toasting fork that used to hang beside the fire and scratch her head with it, but now either her head had ceased to itch or she had mislaid the toasting fork.

Flora spoke in a flat voice, her remarks being addressed invariably to the fire.

'You have cut your hay.'

'Aye.'

'You have stooked it.'

'Aye.'

'Your wife and your daughter helped you.'

'Not my daughter.'

'Your daughter was away on the bus.'

'No, she was out fishing.'

'She caught fish.'

'Aye.'

'You will bring me a fish for my dinner tomorrow.'

'Aye.'

'Sarah, you will cook the fish the way I like it.'

'Aye, sister.'

And so it would go on. She never asked a question and never answered one. She was waited on hand and foot and there appeared to be not a thing organically wrong with her. She was the most uncannily idle and least endearing personality I have met in my life.

Because of Flora, I think, the household was not much visited by the Bruachites, and so until after I had gone to live in my cottage I had not come much into contact with either Sarah or her brother. One dark autumn morning however, when the mists were soaking into the hill tops and the hooded crows were croaking their 'grace before meat', I looked out of my window to see a big strong calf grazing on my croft and trailing behind him what looked like a tangled clothes line. I went out to investigate and the calf, seeing me, started to run away, dragging the clothes line after him. I was horrified to hear a groan. I started forward again cautiously, but again the calf bounded away from me. Sarah's voice from the bundle of clothes came tremulous but clear.

'If I keep a hold of the chain perhaps you could cut the wee bitty rope with a knife.'

I rushed back into the house and got the sharpest knife I could find and as Sarah hauled on the chain I managed to grasp the beast's head rope and slash it quickly. The calf bounded away and I ran to Sarah.

'He pulled up his stake,' she explained. 'And then he got it round my foot and came galloping away down here dragging me after him.' She was half lying on the wet ground, her face chalk white. 'I think the beast has broken my leg for me,' she murmured lucidly and then fainted clean away.

I ran for Yawn and told him what had happened.

'She's broken her leg, you say?' he asked with patent disbelief. Yawn had always regarded me with suspicion; I think he was afraid that I too lurked in caves in stormy weather and might some time beat him to the choicest finds. 'I think so. But do hurry and come and get her.'

'Ach, I suppose I'd best take the wheelbarrow,' he said ungraciously, leaving his half-finished cup of tea. Flora made some derogatory remark in the direction of the fire. I paused for a moment thinking that if I explained Sarah's predicament to her carefully it might rouse her into action and wondered vaguely if she did attempt to rise whether the chair would cling to her back, like the shell of a snail. Her vacant immobility quelled the impulse and I hastened back to Sarah.

'Could we get her to my cottage?' I suggested to Yawn.

He bestowed upon me and my cottage a look that should have annihilated the two of us.

'No,' he replied, 'I'll take her to my own house. I don't suppose there's much wrong with her.'

I hated to see Sarah bundled into a wheelbarrow and

trundled over the rough ground, but I realized that under the circumstances it was the best thing we could do. She obviously must not be left there until neighbours could be recruited to find a stretcher. Had we decided on that course I felt that some tactless souls would have been certain to turn up with the bier from the burial ground. So Yawn struggled and swore his way home while I hovered meekly behind. A scholar on his way to school came running up to us enquiringly and I sent him with a message intentionally to Morag and unintentionally to everyone else in the village. I 'phoned for the doctor, who came and affirmed that Sarah had indeed broken her leg.

Sarah, quite conscious again, sighed with a certain amount of relief at the news. 'It's thankful I am he didn't have the leg right off me,' she said, displaying her left hand minus its thumb which as a young girl she had lost in a similar accident.

'In that case you would have to have a beautiful new wooden one,' I soothed jovially.

'Ach, like that man with the fire brigade,' she rejoined. 'I believe he keeps a wooden leg some place.' She looked up at the doctor anxiously. 'I will be able to walk again, doctor, will I?'

'Of course you will,' he assured her. 'You'll have to rest it for a while but you'll be as good as new in a few weeks' time.'

'I wish you'd cure my corns for me as quickly while you're about it, doctor,' she said wistfully.

'What are you doing with corns, Sarah?' demanded the doctor.

'It's they big boots I have to wear. Yawn won't let me have gumboots, and they're after puttin' terrible corns on my feets.'

'Very well, I'll send you over something for them,' promised the doctor, who was new to Bruach and did not yet know that Sarah's corns were almost as old as her feet.

'I wonder was he just sayin' that about my leg to comfort me?' she asked us dubiously, when he had gone.

'Now, Sarah!' admonished Morag, who had by this time arrived on the scene full of bracing sympathy and competence. 'Why would he say that if he didn't mean it? Sure, she's been a good leg to you all these years and there's no reason for thinkin' she won't be a good leg to you again.'

Sarah nodded slow acquiesence and stroked the broken leg with tender pride.

Despite her age, Sarah's leg did heal in a remarkably short time. While she was incapacitated I visited her often, taking her whenever I could pictures and photographs of the royal family, to whom she was touchingly devoted. So eager was she to hear of royal activities that whenever she could she stationed herself close to the timid-toned old wireless at news bulletin times simply to hear the Queen mentioned. Under her bed she kept several ribbon-tied boxes full to bursting with photographs she had cut from magazines and newspapers for over half a century, and whenever she had the excuse or the opportunity these were brought out and examined lovingly. The Queen Mother and her two daughters she particularly adored. 'Ach, the bonnie wee Scots lassie,' she would croon as she studied a photograph of the Queen Mother, and 'They sweet little darlings,' as she pored over photographs of the Queen and Princess Margaret as children.

When she was not gloating over photographs of royalty Sarah spent her evenings sewing, using, because her eyes were weak and she would not wear glasses, an outsize darning needle which her brother jocularly referred to as a 'boat-hook'. Flora's former mistress had left her trunks of ravishing evening gowns and it was strangely affecting to see Sarah's white head bent over lengths of pink taffeta or blue satin, her stiff, rough fingers stabbing the large needle in and out as she transformed the gowns into what she considered to be suitable day dresses for herself. I have seen her mucking out the cow-byre arrayed in sequin-spangled pink taffeta. I have met her on the hill, her swirling skirt of gold satin pulled high above her thin wool-encased legs which stuck out from her black tackety boots like sticks from a glue-pot. I have watched her winkle picking attired in silver lamé and velvets, reinforced by old meal sacks.

By the time she was on her feet again Sarah and I were close friends. I had taken on the task of writing her letters for her, much to the relief of her brother who disliked letter-writing and considered he had quite enough to do to write his own. I sympathized with Yawn; living in isolated places demands an enormous amount of letter-writing, ranging from ordering a pound of sausages from the butcher to a new dress from the store. Yawn, who I suspected was really very fond of his younger sister though he never allowed his affection to show, had come by this time to accept me as not quite such a menace to his fortunes as he had at first believed. Soon he took to calling in at my cottage and presenting me with some of his trophies: a sisal doormat, which I was very glad to have; tortured lumps of paraffin wax which helped fire-lighting considerably; a life-jacket, and more than once a lump of venison which I had to believe was from a freshly washed-up stag.

'Yawn,' I asked him one day, voicing a fear of my own; 'have you ever come across a body on the shore?'

'Indeed I did once,' he admitted, 'and I was wonderin'' to myself what sort of a beast it was till I saw it was wearin'' socks.'

'I found a baby seal washed up the other day and that was horrid enough,' I said with a shudder. 'It very nearly cured me of beachcombing. I don't know what I'd do if I found a human body.'

'Ach, there's no need to do anythin'' but let the tide take it away again,' he told me. 'We used to get four pounds for them but there's nothin'' in it now.'

He watched me as I nailed an old piece of linoleum to the top of a tea-chest which I hoped to use as a coop for a broody hen.

'She'll no keep chicks warm enough in that,' Yawn pronounced, 'But I have in my shed what will do for you to cover it over. I'll bring some of it with me next time I'm passin'.' A few days later he brought me some suitable lengths of heavy felted material which I draped over the tea-chest.

'What do you call that stuff?' I asked him. 'It seems to

be the ideal thing for the job.'

'Indeed I don't know,' he replied. 'It was just some stuff I got on the shore. In a big sort of tank it was, lots of it. I had Sarah make me a mattress of it and I can tell you I've never laid on a more comfortable bed.' I was dubious of its attractions as a mattress, but thought it possible that Yawn preferred his bed to be as tough and unyielding as himself.

'I doubt you'll have to nail it on for the storms,' he called as he shut the gate behind him.

'I shall probably do that in any case,' I assured him, but lazily left it for another time.

Some days later when Sarah came to have her letters written she brought the news that Yawn was in bed with lumbago. The doctor had sent him some pills but he was to rest in bed for a while.

'And there's the corn half-cut, and the hay still in cocks,' Sarah moaned. 'We'll be gatherin' in the corn at New Year. I can no understand it,' she went on, 'he used to have terrible rheumatics right enough but when once he'd started sleepin' on that new mattress I made him of that stuff he found on the shore he's never felt hardly a twinge.'

Hector and Erchy were persuaded to give a hand with scything corn while Sarah and I gathered and tied it into sheaves, and when it had spent the required three Sundays in the field we stacked it. Yawn was still confined to his bed.

My broody hen had hatched her chicks—three cockerels and two pullets, five out of a setting of a dozen eggs. The rest of the eggs were infertile.

'You'd best get yourself a cockerel that isn't so particular,' said Morag when I told her.

Autumn was bullied out of existence in a single night and when I went the next morning to feed my chickens, which had been growing strongly, I found the felt covering their tea-chest had been blown off and the tea-chest itself turned over. The valiant mother brooded the two remaining chicks in its shelter. I resolved to go to the mainland that day for some nails to secure the felt.

The following morning was bright and, as I now knew, treacherously calm, and after breakfast I collected my nails and a hammer and went off to make for the broody hen the home she deserved. As I went out through the door the policeman, his peaked cap catching the sunlight, was opening the gate.

'You haven't a dog, have you?' he asked.

'No,' I said. 'Why?'

'There's been complaints of sheep worryin' and I'm wantin' to see all the dog licences,' he told me.

He saw my hammer and nails. 'What are you going to do? Building yourself a new house, is it?'

I took him and showed him the tea-chest and the cheeping chicks and the indomitable old mother. His eye lit on the strips of felt that lay in readiness.

'Good God!' he gasped in horror. 'Where did you get that stuff?'

'On the shore,' I replied, a trifle bewildered.

He picked up a piece and examined it very gingerly. He passed his tongue over dry lips.

'What are you thinkin' of doin' with it?'

'Oh, I'm going to nail it to the top of the tea-chest to keep it warm and dry. It's good heavy stuff too, it will add a bit of weight.'

'Like hell you are,' said the policeman. I noticed he had gone pale.

'How much of this stuff have you got?' he demanded.

'Oh, just that you see there.'

'Has anybody else got any?'

'I don't know,' I replied evasively. Yawn would never forgive me if I betrayed the fact that he was sleeping on a mattress of it.

The policeman became authoritative. 'You'll not touch that stuff at all,' he ordered. 'You'll leave it there till I get my instructions what to do with it. I'll go away and 'phone now. Don't you touch it on any account. It's highly dangerous. A find of this kind should have been reported right away.'

'Dangerous?' I echoed incredulously; the stuff looked harmless enough to me. 'Why, what is it?'

'Gun-cotton,' returned the policeman abruptly.

'Good God!' I gasped, even more horror stricken than he had been.

He loped off to where his car was parked and as soon as he was out of sight I flew to Yawn's house in mounting panic. I rushed into the kitchen. Sarah was out and for the only time in my life I had reason to be grateful for the impassivity of the figure beside the fire. It recalled me to my senses.

'Is Yawn in bed?' I asked with enforced calm.

'In bed he is.'

I raised my voice. 'Yawn!' I called. 'May I come in?'

'Come in.' I went through into the bedroom. Yawn was propped up with pillows, placidly smoking his pipe. I was not wholly conversant with the properties of gun-cotton but my stomach nevertheless turned over at the sight of him.

'Yawn,' I began, 'can you get up without help?'

'Ach, no indeed. My back's that bad I canna' even turn myself over. The pain's terrible. Terrible just.'

'Then you'll have to be got up,' I insisted urgently. 'That mattress you're sleeping on . . .'

'Indeed it's a grand mattress right enough,' he interpolated. 'An' I believe it's helpin' a lot to cure me of this lumbago the doctor says I've got. It's doin' more than his pills is doin' for me anyway. I was helpless at first; helpless like a child, but just lying' here in my bed I'm feelin' myself gettin' better every day, though the pain is still awful bad when I move.'

I took a deep breath. 'Yawn,' I enunciated carefully, 'the policeman has just seen some of that stuff your mattress is made of and he tells me it's explosive!'

'Never!' protested Yawn.

'Yes, he's certain it's gun-cotton and highly explosive.'

Yawn's body stiffened and his eyes fixed themselves unwaveringly on my own. He must have seen my panic.

'Get out of the room, woman!' he directed me sternly.

I stood blinking at his tone of voice. 'Get out of the room while I put on my trousers,' he shouted at me. I fled.

Now if any doctor reading this is sceptical about the efficacy of gun-cotton for curing rheumatism and lumbago I should like to assert here and now that within five minutes of acquainting him with the news I saw Yawn outdoing the man of Bethesda; he not only took up his bed but he ran and ran and ran to where his croft ended in a cliff that overhung the sea. He flung the mattress over the edge and then went back to the house where he finished dressing himself. Then he went out to feed the cows. He has never suffered from lumbago or rheumatism since.

Sarah came hurrying back into the kitchen, full of consternation.

'My brother, my brother!' she gasped out. 'What has happened to him?'

I told her.

'Well, well, and wasn't he always after sayin' it was wonderful stuff,' she said.

Flora looked at the fire. 'He is himself again.'

'Aye, sister.'

'He has thrown away his bed.'

'Aye, he has so.' A bawl from a calf took Sarah scurrying outside. Flora wanted to be told why Yawn had thrown away his bed so she repeated her statement.

'He has thrown away his bed.'

'Yes.' The old 'cailleach' was getting no indulgence from me. Her empty eyes slid from the fire to my face and back again. 'It was damp.'

'No, not damp.'

'It was no longer comfortable,' she vouchsafed.

'It had become very uncomfortable indeed,' I agreed, and wished I could ask the policeman to leave me a sample of the gun-cotton to offer her as a cushion.

V. Work on the Croft

THE SKY WAS EFFERVESCING with lark song, the rocky out-crops of the croft were starred with wide-eyed primroses and every convenient wall or hedge near each house was draped with blankets out for their annual sun bath. I sat in my garden trying, very inadequately, to put the tints and demi-tints of the dry-stone byre with its thatched roof, its blue door and its hem of tiring daffodils on to paper, when I heard the voice of Yawn calling to me from the garden gate on which he was leaning with contorted self-possession.

'I was wonderin' would I get a hand to plant the pota-toes,' he asked. 'The tractor says he'll be here at ten o'clock in the mornin'.'

I told him I would certainly help plant his potatoes and carried on with my painting. Yawn, gaining confidence, came into the garden and looked over my shoulder. 'My, but it's mighty like,' he exclaimed with unflattering surprise. I murmured non-committally, being well aware that my artistic skill is negligible. I venture to paint only when I feel compelled to preserve, strictly for my own enjoyment, some scene that I fear I may never see again. In this case I knew that the thatched roof of the byre was rapidly disintegrating and that it must soon be replaced with corrugated iron. I knew too, from shivering experience, that in winter the dry-stone walls merely acted as funnels for arctic draughts and fine snow and that if Bonny were ever to have reasonably comfortable quarters they would have to be mortared and cemented. From the point of picturesqueness I regretted having to replace the thatch, but the prospect of the walls being mortared and thus denying access to all the little birds which nightly shared Bonny's steading was indeed a gloomy one. Admittedly, I rarely glimpsed the birds but, each morning, the stall was so liberally betokened that I knew there must have been at least a dozen of them snug in their secret roosts above Bonny's warm breath. I liked to imagine the night noisy with their cheeped 'gardyloos'.

'You know,' went on Yawn, 'there's some of these painters comes here and sits around for days with their paints and when they show you what they've done you'd not be knowin' whether it was the hills themselves or some cocks of old hay that's been left out in the wet you're lookin' at. Indeed, I've seen my cow paint better pictures with his tail on the back of his stall than some of them. But that,' he made an indulgent gesture towards my pad, 'that's like, right enough.' He watched me for a few moments longer. 'You'll be after wantin' a nice frame for it when you've done,' he suggested.

'Oh no,' I said, and firmly resisting further compliments I put the finished painting inside an old blotter along with several others and dismissed it from my mind.

The following morning again dawned sunlit and light-hearted with a brisk wind that coaxed the ripples of the bay into new-toothed baby smiles and as soon as I heard the noise of the tractor in the distance I pulled on a pair of gumboots and went to join the coterie of people who were already assembled on Yawn's croft. The cultivation of the land in Bruach could not begin until the cattle, which were allowed to graze the crofts from the end of November until the spring, had been driven back again to the hills, and so it was always well into April or even early May before spades were probing into the hoof-pitted ground and 'pliachs' were thrusting through the newly turned soil. There were no tractors in Bruach. Only one man still used the 'cas chrom', the old hand plough. Those who were lucky enough to possess a horse and considerate enough to feed it oats in the winter might be able to use it for the spring ploughing but generally the horses, left to roam the moors wild and unfed throughout the severe winters, were too weak to pull a plough by the time spring came round. For most of the crofters, the only alternative to digging was to await with that peculiar brand of patience inherent in the Gael the arrival of the itinerant Department of Agriculture tractor and, as the tractor's schedule, never a very strict one, was likely to be upset by weather and by mechanical breakdowns so that it might be late in the season before it reached the village, the noise of its approaching engine was always a very welcome sound indeed.

It was the custom for all the would-be hirers of the tractor to band together and help one another with their planting, not only because the tractor was charged by the hour or because of the ever-present fear that the weather might break but because in Bruach potato planting was, curiously enough, traditionally a co-operative task and it was entered into with something like a festival spirit. A string of women and girls, all with bright floral aprons covering their tweed skirts and all gumbooted like myself, were stationed along the plot when I arrived. Others were filling pails and bowls from the sacks of potatoes and fertilizers, their unrestrained chuckling and chattering adding yet more geniality to the day. The men, sombre in comparison yet equally loquacious, were carrying on their backs the last creelfuls of dung to the heaps dotted along the length of the plot. The manipulation of heavy creels of dung requires a certain amount of skill as well as strength. The men first removed their caps to save them from falling off and being buried in the dung and then, as they bent well forward, they jerked up the bottom of the creel from behind so that the contents spilled out over their heads. As every one of the men showed a round, bald patch on his head when he removed his cap I was forced to the conclusion that hair and potatoes do not respond to the same fertilizers. When the tractor was ready to start ploughing, the men, except for Yawn, took forks and plunged them into the heaps of dung and, as the furrow was turned, they threw the dung into it. Yawn followed, placing potatoes at regular intervals on the dung, demonstrating with unspoken authority to the women who followed him how far apart he wished the plants spacing. Those of us who were not planting filled and carried pails of artificial fertilizer and, straggling in the wake of the tractor like dilatory gulls, we circled each potato with a handful of fertilizer. Sarah, who was supposed to be in the kitchen preparing a 'strupak' for everyone, kept scurrying anxiously from the house to inspect progress and to plunge her bare hands deep into a pile of dung to add a couple of handfuls when she feared a potato might suffer from lack of nourishment. She wore a sacking apron over a plum-coloured velvet dress, the deep-hanging sleeves of which were lavishly trimmed with flounces. The flounces were soon showing signs of overnourishment.

When the last sod had been turned and the empty sacks had been shaken out in the breeze, we sat on the grass waiting for the tractor-man and those who had accepted the invitation to a 'strupak' before moving on to a neighbour's planting.

'I could do with a cup of tea myself,' said Erchy, 'but I'm damty sure I'm no goin' to have to talk to old Flora just so as to get it.'

'Nor me either,' panted Anna Vic who, despite her stoutness and the shortness of her breath, was one of the nimblest workers in the village.

'That old cailleach,' went on Erchy with strong disapproval, 'I believe she'd still stay fixed if you snatched the chair from under her.'

'Indeed yes,' echoed Anna Vic, with a giggle. 'Sarah was around at our own house the other night askin' would she get a broody hen so she could hatch out some chicks. I hadn't one, so I told her she should try puttin' a clutch of eggs under Flora to see what would happen.' She laughed apologetically.

'I believe they would have hatched too,' said Erchy, 'but I doubt you'd never be able to find the chicks supposin' they did. Not till they was grown hens anyway.'

'Aye, but, poor soul, it must be awful sittin' there with nothin' to look foward to from one year to another.'

'Nothin' but gettin' the flu' every winter,' corrected Erchy.

When the village potato planting was finished the tractor started to plough for corn. I was fortunately able to grow enough potatoes in my garden for my own requirements and also to provide Bonny with her evening mash of boiled potatoes dried off with oatmeal, which is the nightly fare of a cosseted Hebridean cow, but I yearned to see some of the matted turf of my croft turned into black earth to match the crofts of my neighbours and so I resolved to try growing a patch of oats. I had already learned how to tie and stook corn from helping Morag and I was fairly certain that I should be able to get someone to come and cut it for me when it was ready. So the tractor came and ploughed and Peter, always fiercely eager to oblige, came and broke down the sods by harnessing himself to some home-made harrows and dragging them over and over the plot. To the casual observer the sowing of oats looks ridiculously easy and when I used to hear Morag importuning various male relatives to come and sow corn for her I used to wonder why such an independent old woman did not undertake the task herself. Whenever there was an opportunity I watched the sowers at work. They appeared to do nothing more strenuous or scientific than to walk steadily up and down the plot scattering handfuls of seed from the pouch full of grain which they wore as a sling over one shoulder. I evaded acceptance of Yawn's offer without committing myself to a definite refusal and, tying an old sheet over my shoulder and filling the pouch of it with grain, I went forth sowing. It was not long before I began to suspect that there was a good deal more to sowing corn than there had always looked to be. I paused to survey my work. In some parts of the plot the grain lay almost as thick as it lay in my pouch: in others it was as scant as if I had aimed each seed singly, like a dart at a dartboard. I gave up when I had covered a few more square yards without noticeable improvement in my aim and as soon as dusk came I surreptitiously forked earth over my efforts and humbly approached Yawn, who came the following day.

'I see you've been after tryin' to do it for yourself,' he rebuked me, for the birds had traitorously uncovered my attempts at concealment.

'Yes, I did, as a matter of fact,' I admitted with limp gaity. 'It always looks so simple when other people do it.'

Yawn grunted and started to sow, the grain scattering from each effortless swing of his arm with the conscientious regularity of spray from a watering can.

'I wish you'd tell me the secret of getting the seed to fall so regularly,' I said.

Yawn retorted with another grunt.

'Is there a special way of sowing so that the seed falls so regularly?' I persisted, for in spite of having tried and failed, it still looked remarkably easy.

'Yes, there is,' said Yawn reluctantly, not lifting his eyes from the ground. 'You must always see that you throw it five grains to the horse's hoof-mark,' an instruction which, considering the ground had been ploughed by tractor and harrowed by Peter, wearing gumboots, was only faintly enlightening. I stood watching him perplexedly while the shadows of gulls' wings passed unconcernedly over the plot. In the early morning the gulls would be stuffing themselves on the grain, abortively it seemed, for the locals maintained that the birds could not digest the grain and vomited it shortly after eating it. Still baffled by Yawn's technique I left him absorbed in his task while I went to put on the kettle for his 'strupak'. When I returned he had finished sowing and was himself watching Peter who had brought his graipe and was forking over the seed.

'You could get a sub-side-y on this ploughin',' Yawn told me. 'There's not been a plough on this croft for years and there's a good grant for it.'

'Oh, I hardly think it worth while,' I said. 'It's such a small plot.'

'Indeed, it's no small at all. I believe it's the same size near enough to my own piece and that's near an acre.'

'An acre? Not that plot we were planting the other day with potatoes behind the tractor?'

'Aye, that one.'

'That was never an acre, Yawn, or anything like it,' I contradicted flatly, after a swift mental rehearsal of the table of square measure.

Yawn turned on me a withering look that gradually grew less withering as he realized I might possibly know what I was talking about. 'Well,' he conceded with lofty defiance, 'it was an acre long anyway.' He stalked away crossly, not waiting for his cup of tea, but a day or two later when he had forgiven me for being right and wished to make amends he was back again at my door with a parcel under his arm.

'I have but what'll do a nice frame for the picture you were paintin',' he said. 'I got it washed up on the shore a day or two back just. It's lost its picture and I've had to put a wee bit board on the back and this bit chain I had by me to hang it. See and get your picture now and we'll try will it fit.'

Feeling rather touched by his thoughtfulness I went into the bedroom and got my painting and when I came back into the kitchen Yawn had unwrapped the parcel and was proudly holding up a very distinctive horseshoe-shaped frame enamelled in turquoise blue. I stifled an incredulous gasp and watched his face intently as he carefully inserted the picture between the backing and the frame. I swear there was no trace of guile in his expression. 'There now,' he said, holding it up for my inspection. 'Do you not think that looks fine now?'

With a tremulousness that he fortunately took to be modesty I agreed that it did indeed.

'It makes all the difference to a picture to put it in a nice frame,' he told me. 'Now, where would you like it hangin' and I'll put a nail in for you while I'm here?' I indicated a spot in the darkest corner of the room. 'Ach, but it'll no catch the light there at all. Folks will not see it there.'

'It's not a very good painting,' I demurred.

'Ach, it's no bad. No bad at all. What about havin' it here?' He held it up on the wall above the cooker. 'See now, there's a nail here all ready for it.' Silently I cursed the obstinancy of that one nail. Yawn stepped back to admire the effect. 'Beautiful just,' he commented. I echoed his admiration. 'I knew as soon as I saw the frame lyin' there on the shore that it was just the proper frame for your picture,' he assured me with solemn affability as he hurriedly took his leave, no doubt to escape the profuseness of my gratitude. Dear Yawn. How shocked he would have been had he suspected the double entendre of his last remark. But if anyone between here and America happens to have lost a turquoise blue enamelled lavatory seat they might be interested to know that it hangs in my kitchen above the cooker framing an amateurish representation of an old stone byre with a decaying thatched roof and a hem of tired daffodils. It looks beautiful just!

As spring advanced and the days lengthened to accommodate all the extra work it brought, peats were cut and dried and stacked; cows calved. Normally Bruach cows were left out on the hill to calve where they chose, the calves being left to run with their mothers until the rounding up for the autumn sales but, when the date for Bonny's calving drew close, Morag, who had never ceased to be as watchful over my interests as her own, advised me to bring her into the croft so that I should be able to keep an eye on her.

'You mind yon trouble our own Ruari had with his bought in heifer,' she cautioned.

I remembered the trouble very well. One evening whilst I was still living with Morag, Bella, Ruari's shy and untranquil wife, had rushed round calling distractedly for Morag to come and help because their new heifer was 'stuck up with his calf'. I was implored to go and 'phone for the vet. Some hours later, when I was sitting in my own room with my knitting and my nightcap of cider, I heard a knock on the door and one of the young village boys put his head round and said, with perfect seriousness: 'Morag's wantin' a clean sheet for the calf's bed.'

I could only echo his request uncomprehendingly.

'Aye, she's sayin' you will get one from the drawer up in the wee room.'

For a few moments I stared at the boy, trying to reconcile my knowledge of Bruach calf pens with the likelihood of a calf being put to bed in clean sheets in one of them. Deciding that the boy was probably playing some game of 'dare and do' and I was the chosen dupe, I grinned and relaxed into my chair.

'She's wantin' it right away if you'll give it to me.' The boy's voice was edged with intolerance.

'Are you sure it has to be a clean sheet?' I mocked, fully

expecting to hear a burst of giggling from his cronies who I felt sure were bolstering him with their presence out there in the dark.

'Yes indeed.' his expression grew tense as I still made no attempt to go upstairs. 'Must I go back and tell her you'll no give me a sheet then?' he demanded testily. 'Will I tell her she must come and get it for herself?'

Against my better judgement I went up to the wee room and taking a fresh-laundered sheet from the drawer I thrust it into his waiting hands, resigning myself to the fact that if it was a hoax it would be all over the village by morning. I could, of course, have gone over to Ruari's and made discreet enquiries but as my presence would doubtless have added to the complexities of the situation it seemed unfair to pester them with my doubts. Morag had still not returned when I went to bed that night and the next morning when she brought in my breakfast she was looking as dishevelled as if she had spent the night outdoors in a gale of wind.

'Well, Ruari has a fine bull calf for himself after all the trouble,' was her greeting. I murmured suitably, waiting for the teasing which I was sure would soon begin. 'An' fancy Bella never havin' a clean sheet that would do the calf's bed,' she exclaimed disgustedly.

I answered her with a look of easily simulated amazement.

'Wasn't all she could find an old cover that the colours leaked out of when it got wet,' she enlarged. 'It would never have done for the beast. I would have been ashamed of myself.' She shook her head sadly over her sister-in-law's shortcomings.

'I thought the boy was playing a hoax on me when he came and asked for a clean sheet for the calf's bed,' I confessed ruefully.

'You did? Right enough he told me you didn't seem as if you wanted to give it to him. Why was that now?'

'I just couldn't imagine a calf being put to bed between sheets,' I told her. 'I still can't. It sounds so utterly unlikely.'

Morag suppressed a snigger. 'But, mo ghaoil, a calf's bed is what the beast lies in before he's born. What would be the English for it now?'

'The womb, you mean?'

'Aye, right enough, the womb. Well, that came away with the calf last night and we had to try would we push it back in again with a sheet. Some folk use a bag of straw but Ruari, he would have none of it. A clean sheet, he said, and nothin' else it had to be.' As she went into more gruesome details I realized that my appetite for breakfast—haggis and egg—was wilting rapidly.

'And you say everything's all right now?' I cut in desperately.

'Ach, aye. The vet had to do a wee operation on the calf but this mornin' when I sees him he was skippin' around on his legs as though there'd never been a thing wrong with him.' She poured herself a cup of tea and sat down. 'My, but that vet was tired before he was finished and that was at the back of four this mornin'.'

'It was a bitterly cold night too for this time of year,' I said, mentally experiencing the discomforts of the average Bruach byre.

'Aye, we was all complainin' of the cold though the vet was sayin' he was warm enough where he was.' She ended in a little hiccough of laughter.

'Why, where was that?' I asked innocently.

'Half-way inside the cow for the best part of the time, mo ghaoil,' she informed me with great relish.

So Bonny awaited her confinement on the comparative lushness of the croft, becoming more of a household pet daily. She was the nearest thing to the real old Highlander it had been possible for me to buy: shaggy, red-haired, with a black-ringed snout. Her horns were crooked.

'One of her horns points to heaven and the other to hell,' my neighbours said when they saw her. 'You'll find she's half angel and half devil.' But she was mostly angel. I could perhaps have regularized her appearance if I had taken Morag's advice which was to bake a large turnip in the hot peat ashes and clap it quickly on to the crooked horn, gradually coaxing it into position as it softened. I doubted if Bonny would take kindly to the treatment and secretly I was glad of her cock-eyed appearance because it made her more easily distinguishable from the scores of other Highland cattle out on the hill. I had embarrassed memories of volunteering to feed Morag's cows and of standing calling forlornly in the gathering dusk unable to tell one cow from another, until one of them had had the good sense to recognize me.

When Bonny did calve she accomplished it uneventfully. I went to pay her my usual morning visit and found she had a tiny replica of herself snuggling into her flank.

Her eyes were dark and dilated with love and she lowed softly as I approached, but though she shook her wide horns at me in a cautionary way when I started to fondle the calf she was careful to ensure that they did not touch me. The first thrill of having a croft of my own had come when I held in my hand the first warm egg from my hens. Then had come the acquisition of Bonny; the first turned earth, and now Bonny's calf which was a sturdy little thing with a tightly curled light brown coat that reminded me of aerated chocolate.

Once all the village cows had calved, milk, which was always scarce in winter, became super-abundant. Crowdie was offered with every strupak and cream was not only served at every meal but was smoothed on the skin as an emollient for sunburn. As the days grew warmer and we discarded winter coverings, the clegs became aggressively familiar; weeds seemed to appear in full stature overnight, imperilling the young potato plants; the grass on the crofts grew long enough to ripple in the wind; the midges which outrival Glasgow bread and lavish Public Assistance as the curse of the Highlands, came in their hordes, vanquishing the clegs no doubt in the manner of 'greater fleas,' and tormented us as we hoed and earthed up our potatoes. The rainy spell of July came and went leaving behind it a lush carpet of growth that effectively camouflaged the stony soil and when, just about the time in English churches the harvest festival hymns were being rehearsed, scythes were brought out and sharpened: the hay harvest had begun.

All hay in Bruach was cut with scythes by the men. The

spreading and cocking being left to the women and children until the hay was cured and ready to be built into winter stacks when the men again took charge. I had learned to scythe inexpertly but I could not keep up the steady swing hour after hour which is necessary to cut an appreciable amount of hay. If I were not to have to buy in for Bonny's winter feeding I had to have help. Erchy, on whom I could always rely for croft work, cut most of the hay aided by oft-promised, perfunctory and Morag-goaded assistance from Hector, but even so I began to find the spreading, raking, turning, cocking and re-spreading every fine morning rather more than I could manage alone. I discovered to my dismay that I was lagging behind my neighbours and though everyone assured me periodically that there was no hurry because haymaking could go on until the New Year if necessary, I went to see Peter's mother, Sheena, to ask if she could spare him to help me sometimes.

Sheena and Peter, though they worked the croft adjoining my own, lived at the farther end of the village. Sheena was old, totteringly agile, but thoroughly indomitable and she managed to keep Peter who, despite his simple-mindedness, was possessed of exuberant strength and wayward fancies, in complete subjection. Her home with its heavy-lidded thatched roof was one of the oldest in the village and her dim kitchen exuded friendliness as uninterruptedly as its sagging stove exuded smoke. The door was open, letting the blue peat smoke, tinged with the smell of newly scorched flour, breathe out into the serenity of the evening air and I waited for a few moments before making my presence known, listening to Sheena reading aloud to Peter from the newspaper in a halting baritone. She jumped up as she heard my voice, dragged me inside and bustled around in her stockinged feet making a 'strupak', pausing every now and then to clap me on the shoulder to tell me how hardy I was and to ask Peter if she had not been saying to him just that day how she loved me like a sister. She began rooting under the recess bed in the corner of the room and disinterred a brown paper parcel tied with string. I realized with despair that I was once again going to have to swallow a piece of special presentation shortbread which Sheena had once been sent from Edinburgh and which she had since hoarded for honoured guests. The firm claimed on their tins to have been making the shortbread for over a century and when, on the occasion of my very first visit to Sheena, I had unsuspectingly accepted a piece, I was immediately convinced that Sheena's tin was one of the original ones. Since then, despite repeated invitations and a genuine affection on my part for the old lady, I had purposely made my visits rare ones, always in the hope that enough honoured guests had called on her meantime to ensure my never being offered the shortbread again. It appeared, however, that the supply was inexhaustible and I wondered how many more tins reposed in the scarcely explored territory beneath the bed. Sheena's eyesight was poor and I could easily have secreted the shortbread in my pocket had it not been for Peter, whose gaze followed my every movement like that of a mesmerized sparrow.

'Peter, take your stare off Miss Peckwitt this minute!'

Sheena admonished him and thrusting the newspaper into his hands with a gesture that made him wince she bade him look at the pictures. Peter obliged with goggling eagerness until his mother, suddenly suspicious, looked over his shoulder and snatched a double page of bathing beauty photographs from him and substituted a veterinary catalogue. Above its staid pages Peter's gaze fastened despairingly on my feet. Peter's habit of staring fixedly at me was one of the most disconcerting things I had to endure. Though I had lived in Bruach for some years I was acutely aware that my activities were still a source of unflagging interest to the inhabitants but they at least watched me covertly. Peter had not the wit to conceal his curiosity and whenever I appeared in sight he became so obsessed with watching me that he completely forgot whatever he was doing until his mother reminded him of it by boxing his ears. Though his attention was embarrassing the inevitable result was that watching Sheena and Peter trying to work together whenever I was at all visible was as entertaining as the antics of a couple of members of the Crazy Gang. Only that afternoon I had gone out to turn my hay and Peter, who had until then been steadily raking hay while his mother gathered it, suddenly caught sight of me. Immediately his raking had become so wildly abandoned that he had raked poor Sheena's tottery legs from under her and tumbled her into the hay before her shouts had penetrated his excitement and he had stopped long enough to allow her to pick herself up and rush at him to box his ears. The previous day they had been building a cock in a rising wind and Sheena had been running here and there gathering up bundles of hay in her arms and bringing them into the lee of the cock. So tired was she and so intent on getting the job finished that not for some time had she noticed that Peter, whose eyes of course were fixed undeviatingly on me engaged on a similar task, was grabbing each bundle of hay as she brought it and was flinging it ecstatically to the top of the cock so that the wind caught it and scattered it again for Sheena to gather afresh.

After the necessary preliminaries had been gone through I made known to Sheena the purpose of my visit.

'An' indeed Peter shall come and help you, mo ghaoil. Indeed he shall. He's a good boy though he is what you say in the English, "softly up the stairs". But you shall have him with pleasure, Miss Peckwitt. Just as soon as he can be spared from our own hay.' She did not consult Peter. 'An' he loves you, Miss Peckwitt,' she continued ardently. 'Is that not true, Peter? Are you not after tellin' me near every day how much you love Miss Peckwitt?' Peter nodded startled but vigorous acquiescence and under cover of their protestations I thankfully transferred the piece of shortbread to my pocket and embarked upon a fresh-baked girdle-scone, the appetizing smell of which had been filling the kitchen when I had first arrived. I cut short what seemed to be developing into a panegyric on my attractions and Peter's abilities by complimenting Sheena on her scones.

'Ach, mo ghaoil, but I threw them together just when I came in from the hay for the bread had grown such a beard with the mould that was on it. Indeed, I was sayin' to Peter it looked just like myself after yon hot spell we was havin'.' She struck her mouth with her hand. 'Ach, but I wish I had the right words and I could tell you. I could make you laugh if I had more English,' she said regretfully.

'But you are always making me laugh, Sheena,' I answered with perfect truthfulness.

'Well, glad I am to hear it, mo ghaoil, for laughter is as good for folks as a plate of porridge, and just like porridge everybody should have some every day.' She squeezed my shoulder emphatically. 'Well, I was tellin' you, my face got that sore with the sun and the wind that I just splathered the cream I'd been savin' for the butter on it and I sat out at the front of the house in the shade for I was gaspin' like the birds with the heat. I must have fallen asleep for mercy!, when I woke up and put a hand to my face it was covered with hair like a goat's. "Here," says I to myself, "what in the world has happened to me?" But then I see the hairs has come off in my hand.' She laughed noiselessly. 'What did I find with it all that my fine fellow Peter here was after tryin' would he cut his hairs and he'd had to come and sit out beside myself to do it, and the wind had blown his hairs all over my face so that the cream had stickled them.' She had been squeezing and patting my shoulder repeatedly while she was relating the incident and when she had finished she bent herself double with spasms of laughter that had worn themselves to shreds before they reached her throat. I laughed delightedly at her story but Peter, no doubt remembering the punishment he had received on that occasion, only watched his mother warily. 'Ach, mo ghaoil, but if only you had more of the Gaelic, I could tell you better the sight I looked,' she lamented again. So I laughed immoderately to please her.

The kitchen darkened as the sky composed itself for rain and stray drops came down the chimney to sizzle on the warm stove.

'That old chimbley never did keep out the piss properly at all,' Sheena explained pleasantly.

'Well,' I said, getting up from my chair, 'I suppose we really need the rain.'

'Right enough we do,' she replied. 'Indeed, did you ever feel weather as hot as it was this last week or two back?' she demanded hoarsely.

'It certainly was hot,' I admitted.

'My, but poor Peter's that burned through his shirt workin' in the hay that he's after goin' every few minutes to rub himself on the dyke the same as the cattles with the itchin' it's givin' him.' I caught a look of desperate appeal from Peter in time to stifle the sceptical comment I was about to make on the possibility of the sun burning through the thick flannel shirts which Peter wore perennially and recalled having seen him basking shirtless on a secluded part of the shore the previous Sunday when no doubt his mother had believed him to be in church.

I said I must go before the rain became heavy and Sheena, leaving Peter sitting in the deep gloom of the unlit kitchen, escorted me part way along the road, asseverating earnestly that 'the first fine day after the next,' I would get

Peter for my hay if the Lord spared us all. She had not put on a jacket to accompany me and I pressed her to return home before she got too wet.

'Ach, a little rain will never wet me, mo ghaoil,' she asserted airily, but nevertheless she allowed me to go on alone. It was not until she turned away that I noticed she was still in her stockinged feet!

The rain continued all night, making it impossible to work in the hay the next morning, and I resolved to try to catch up on some of my house cleaning which had been neglected for the urgency of hay-making. I had just started to polish the floor when Sarah came to tell me that Bonny was bulling. She advised me strongly to take her to the bull straight away. I quailed at the thought of taking Bonny within a mile of any bull.

'Would Yawn take her for me?' I asked hopefully.

'Yawn would take her right enough but he's away on the bus this mornin'. His brother's havin' a funeral to himself today,' she explained.

Erchy and Hector would, I knew, be too busy with tourists and even if there had been no tourists Hector would have been too busy with all the pretty girl relatives who were staying in the village. I could not go to Sheena and ask for Peter because she had never permitted him officially to know the facts of life. I had to reconcile myself to the fact that if I was to have milk next summer I must take Bonny to the bull myself.

Long ago, when I had first come to Bruach, I had once encountered a large, shaggy, Highland bull standing in the middle of the high road with 'Monarch of the Glen' impassivity and I had, some time later, been an astonished witness to the spectacle of a young girl coming up behind the bull, slapping its rump with her bare hand and commanding it to 'get on there!' The bull had trotted off obediently! When I had come out of my petrified trance and the telephone kiosk in which I had taken refuge at first sight of the bull, I had determined that someday I myself would do, or try to do, exactly as that young girl had done. It was a resolution which seemed destined to remain unfulfilled, perhaps because it has subsequently been my misfortune always to meet my bulls face to face, a situation which is intimidating enough to wilt far less feeble spirits than mine. Now, on Bonny's behalf, I must go and scrape acquaintance with one. I led the docile Bonny on a short length of rope, experiencing increasingly the sensation that my torso was trying to disclaim kinship with my legs. At Morag's I called in, partly for a brief respite, partly to enquire whether she could tell me the bull's whereabouts.

'Surely, mo ghaoil, but it's lucky you are. He's away tomorrow in the float and Angus has him in on the croft till the lorry will come and get him. You'll only need to take the beast there.'

Fiona, Hector and Behag's little daughter, started to pull on her gumboots busily.

'Where do you think you're goin', Fiona?' asked Behag, with motherly indulgence.

'I'm away to take Miss Peckwitt to the bull,' announced Fiona firmly and neither Morag nor Behag appeared to find her intention at all extraordinary. Behag was always content to have Fiona in my company because apparently I was the only guardian the child did not try to elude. Fiona was a born roamer and tended to disappear for hours even when a strict eye was being kept on her. She was also the most intractable, unquenchable little bundle of independence I have ever come across and I most emphatically did not want her company today.

'No, Fiona,' I said. 'You can't come today.'

Fiona ignored my refusal and struggled with childish maladroitness into a cardigan.

'You heard Miss Peckwitt say you were not to go,' said Behag, with a helpless look at me and Morag.

'I'm away with her,' said the child imperturbably.

'Fiona!' interjected Morag sternly.

The only sign Fiona gave of having heard was to tighten her lips.

'You must stay with Aunty and Mummy today,' I told her, infusing decision into my voice. 'I'll take you for a walk tomorrow.'

Fiona's grey eyes regarded me implacably. 'I'm comin' with you,' she announced. 'Hurry now!'

Morag gave me an apple as consolation. Fiona demanded one also and she had eaten hers almost before we were back on the road again.

'I'll put your apple in my pocket for you,' she offered insistently as she threw away her own core; 'you can tell me when you don't want it.'

The sun had broken through the cloud to disperse the

dampness of the morning and it grew hot on our backs as we climbed the stony track; flies buzzed around my head incessantly, pestering me only a little more than Fiona's unceasing questions. I was thankful for the temporary distraction of Angus's dogs racing to meet us as we reached the house where Angus's wife apologized for the absence of her husband and also for being unable to accompany us. She was leaning heavily on a stick, having, she said, cut her knee that badly she couldn't put her leg under her. The bull, she told us, was away down in the far park, a fact which, judging from her sudden interest, Bonny had already discovered for herself. She bawled and tugged at her head rope, dragging me after her. There came an answering bawl from the bull and when we reached the gate of the park I let go her rope and drove her speedily through, closing the gate firmly after her.

Bonny stood coquettishly; the bull came cantering towards her. I lay on my stomach on a stony hillock at a safe distance outside the fence and waited, content to study all the secret things among the heather that only the lazy know. The clouds had finally yielded to the sun and the air was full of summery noises: the drawled comments of leisured gulls; the preoccupied hum of insects; the sibilance of the sea. My attention was concentrated on a brilliant green caterpillar ingesting a leaf when suddenly Fiona's voice broke into my absorption with shattering scorn.

'That's the silliest bull I ever see in my life,' she said.

Her interest in the proceedings was slightly embarrassing.

'Fiona,' I cooed, 'come and see the way this caterpillar

is eating his dinner.' The lure was quite ineffective.

'That bull is a silly bull,' she repeated scathingly. 'That's not what he's supposed to do. Take a look will you?' She pulled impatiently at my shoulder.

I turned round. Bonny was standing happily chewing her cud while the bull, with his tail thrashing ecstatically, was down on his forelegs like a calf sucking contentedly at her udder. I stood up and Bonny turned on me a look that was eloquent of bewilderment and pleading.

'What will you do?' demanded Fiona.

'Wait and see,' I said crossly, and stepping over the fence I gave the bull a series of slaps on his rump. 'Get on with you!' I yelled at him, but not waiting to test his obedience I climbed nimbly back over the fence where, shaken by my own audacity, I clung panting to a fence post.

'That's shown him,' shrilled Fiona with untrammelled approbation. She turned to the bull. 'Why did you no do that before, you silly old thing!' she screamed at him derisively.

There was still a long afternoon left for working in the hay when I returned with Bonny so, after a hasty lunch, I went out and began shaking some of the dry hay from the smaller cocks into bigger ones. Peter, at work with his mother on their own croft, was picking the 'stickybuds' (burdocks) out of the hay and, catching sight of me, he flourished a large bunch of them in rapturous greeting. Sheena, who had been bending beside him, straightened herself just as his arm was descending from the greeting. The bunch of burdocks fastened themselves tenaciously to the old grey head. Peter's hands went to his mouth as he saw what he had accomplished. Sheena stood stupefied for a moment and then her hands went slowly up to her own head to assess the damage and then swiftly to Peter's head to administer a flurry of sharp slaps. So much achieved, the two retired to the dyke while Peter did his trembling best to extract the burdocks. For a long and clamorous time the operation continued until finally all the burdocks were removed. Poor Sheena remained seated dejectedly on the dyke but Peter, recovering from the strain of his ministrations, started to re-gather the offending burdocks. I wanted to persuade Sheena to come and have a quiet cup of tea with me to restore her spirits and with this intention I crossed the croft towards the dyke. Peter, whose attention had been temporarily torn from me, became aware of my approach and in a spasm of delight he flung the burdocks he had re-gathered over his shoulder. I gasped. Sheena screamed huskily. Peter turned round and his mouth dropped open as he saw what he had again accomplished. He took to his heels. Sheena, jumping up, tried to totter after him, calling his name savagely but, fearful of her wrath, he kept on running, with only an occasional backward glance. Sheena's hands went up to her twice-tortured head.

'God and Miss Peckwitt forgive me,' she said with both tears and anger shaking her voice, 'but I'm goin' to make a swear.'

And she did.

VI. *The Tinkers*

'SURE WITH THE SPRING they'll be here like the spiders,' said Morag emphatically.

She was speaking of the tinkers, those good-humoured, garrulous itinerants of the Hebrides who annually invaded the village, if not with the first breath of spring then very soon after its first pant, arriving about the same time as the young divinity students who spent their vacations peddling bibles and religious books to the crofting communities—an occupation which made sense of carrying coals to Newcastle—and taking the opportunity to do a little door-to-door evangelism. The crofters placated both by their patronage but for sheer entertainment value, the divinity students were simply not in the same class as the tinkers.

The attitude of the crofters to the tinkers, or 'tinks' as they are more often known, was both interesting and amusing. They despised them, they feared them, yet they welcomed them. They despised them because of the impermanence of their homes which ranged from sod huts to the backs of lorries; I sometimes thought that if Lord Nuffield had turned up in Bruach in a caravan he would have been labelled a 'tink'! They feared them because of a lingering belief in their supernatural powers; they welcomed them because, after the isolation of the winter, any visitors were preferable to no visitors, and the tinks with their gossip and their jokes leavened many a dreary hour. In addition to pots and pans, their multifarious bundles offered for many the only chance of personal shopping, so the crofters were prepared to open wide their doors and watch indulgently while their kitchen tables were transformed into miniature bargain counters and the ragamuffins of the road became high-pressure salesmen.

I wanted to buy a milk pail, hence my interest in the coming of the tinkers. Before Bonny had calved, I had equipped myself with all the paraphernalia necessary for providing a supply of milk, butter and crowdie, i.e. setting bowls, milk sieve, butter pats, etc., but some aberration had made me omit to buy a milk pail. There was no way of remedying the omission until I could get to the mainland and I was reduced meantime to milking into a shallow pudding basin which necessitated either my holding the basin in one hand while I milked with the other—a hand-cramping procedure—or else putting the basin on the ground and risking Bonny's using it as a foot-bath—a mishap which occurred all too frequently.

It was after just such a mishap one day when I was carrying a foot-bath of dung-mottled milk to the half-dozen hens, who now queued with disheartening expectancy whenever I went to milk, that Morag, who never used a gate or a path if she could insinuate herself into the garden any other way, emerged from round the back of the byre.

'Look at that,' I said, showing her the bowl. 'It's the third time this week this has happened. I do wish I could get hold of a proper milk pail.'

It was then that she had told me of the imminent arrival of the tinkers.

'I was hearin' of tinks in Neabost last week,' she reported a few days later. I said I must look out for them.

'You mind,' she said, 'yon collapsible lookin' tink that's always comin' from together in the middle?' I nodded, instantly recognizing the man from her description.

'Well it's himself has the best milk pails, but see now and don't let him charge you more than half a crown for it. I doubt he'll try and get more from you seeing you're a stranger to him, but don't give it to him. Half a crown's what I always pay for them myself.'

Though I had often eavesdropped on my landlady's bargaining with the tinkers I had always been too mistrustful to buy anything from them myself, but when a few days after my conversation with Morag the collapsible tink came gangling happily up my garden path with his shirt gaping out of his trousers, his arms encrusted with shining new milk pails, I greeted him with a welcoming smile and a proffered half-crown.

'I'll take one of your milk pails,' I offered.

Courteously he removed his woebegone felt hat, the band of which was decorated with freshly picked briar roses and bluebells. 'It is a glorious day, madam,' he reproved me gently.

I recollected myself. Even with tinks the politenesses must be first observed. I agreed that it was a glorious day.

'Indeed, but you're badly needin' some rain hereabouts all the same,' he went on conversationally.

'We certainly do,' I said with mounting impatience. I wanted to get back to my goulash which was exasperatedly sizzling its need for attention. Perhaps he too heard the sizzling for he suddenly changed his manner.

'You'd like one of my pails, madam, did you say?'

'Yes, please.' I again held out the half-crown.

'The price is five shillings,' he said smoothly.

I remembered my instructions. 'I'll give you half a crown and no more,' I said.

'I'm sorry, madam, these pails are five shillings. I cannot sell them for half a crown.'

'Half a crown,' I repeated firmly, knowing that if once I gave the tinkers the impression that I was easy game they would never cease their pestering.

Spurning further argument temporarily, he turned his attention to the garden where the young shrubs I had planted were pregnant with blossom and the daffodils had already tired themselves out with the exuberance of their blooming.

'I mind you planting these when I was passin' this way

last year,' he observed affably. I have never discovered if tinkers really do have phenomenal memories or if their assertions are just an astute combination of guesswork and glibness. But they seem to remember everything—always.

' 'Tis wonderful,' he mused on, 'how things grow in a year just.'

I agreed rather shortly. The goulash was definitely singeing but I was reluctant to take my eyes off the tinker for one moment. I wanted my milk pail and to be rid of him.

'And your cow?' he asked as he caught sight of Bonny grazing placidly amidst the blue smoky drifts of bluebells. 'My, my, but that beast has grown too—in just a year now. Can you believe it?' He shook his head wonderingly.

'I didn't have her a year ago,' I pointed out.

'Oh, no, you didn't, but I saw her last spring at the place you got her from and she's grown just,' he retaliated nimbly. 'Does she give plenty milk?'

'Over a gallon, morning and evening,' I told him, 'and I've only a shallow bowl to milk into.'

'In that case you're badly needin' one of my pails, madam.' He lifted his eyes contemplatively to the rumpled peaks of the hills showing above the roof of the byre.

Oh Lord, I thought, now we begin all over again. 'That's right,' I conceded.

Slipping a pail from the bunch on his arm he handed it to me. I examined it perfunctorily and with a smirk of triumph handed him the money. He smiled too. Indeed, I do not think he had ceased to smile during the length of our bargaining, but now there was an added glint in his eye. Giving me a whimsical little nod he pushed the half-crown back into my hand. 'Keep that, madam,' he said chummily. 'Keep it till next year, see will it grow any bigger.'

'Here, no!' I expostulated, but he was already on his way to the gate.

'It's all right, madam.' He paused to pull himself together in the middle. 'I'll be callin' on you again next spring and it's wonderful just what a year can do to make things grow. You'd scarce believe it.'

I was too discomfited to do anything but stand and watch him sauntering his tuneful way back along the road. When I returned to my goulash it was nearly charcoal.

That same evening I called on Morag. There was a shining new milk pail decorating her dresser.

'How much did you pay for this?' I asked.

'Only five shillings,' she said.

'Only five shillings! But you insisted that I mustn't pay more than half a crown, Morag,' I protested fretfully.

'Oh, right enough, mo ghaoil, so I did, but you see these pails is twice the size of the one's he usually brings. I wouldn't have the cheek to expect one of these for half a crown. It would be cheating the man.'

After enduring twelve months of self-torture I opened the door one spring day to 'collapsible'. He still gaped distressingly amidships, his hat was again decorated with flowers, but this time he carried only two milk pails on his arm. Evidently trade had been brisk. He greeted me like an old and valued friend, and began complimenting me on the growth of my garden . . . on the growth of my cow . . . I rushed indoors for my purse and of course found that I had nothing less than a ten-shilling note. I thrust it at him. He was sorry, he said, he had no change; he was more than sorry, he said, he couldn't offer me either of his pails instead of change because they were already ordered. He was sorry. . . . Oh, well! It was worth it really.

Once the tink season had started we had no alternative but to submit to their importuning, for rarely indeed did a week go by without a bevy of tinks descending upon us.

'Indeed what did I find when I got back home from my holiday but five shiny new kettles on the mantelpiece,' complained lame Annie to me as we walked up to the post office together, she to draw her National Assistance. 'And because five different tinks called and them havin' nothin' but kettles to sell just. Jonathon's that soft he couldn't say no to one of them.'

I perforce had to harden my heart even to the extent of resisting 'Aberdeen Angus', the pathetic little Indian whose spotless white turban was always protected from the rain by a plastic bag. Each spring he tottered to our doors, so weighed down on either side by heavy suitcases that he looked to be in imminent danger of splitting down the middle. Mainly because of his skill in reading tea-leaves he was enormously popular despite the exorbitant prices he asked, yet when one saw him leaving the village he still tottered under the weight of his much depleted suitcases.

'Aberdeen Angus' was easily dismissed; he bestowed the same adoring smile on everyone whether or not they refused to purchase. It was not so easy to repulse the elderly female tinks who swung their unconstrained way up to my cottage to extol with soft-spoken persistency the quality of men's shirts, combinations, towels, ladies' dresses and underwear which spilled on to the step from their tablecloth-wrapped bundles. When at last they could bring themselves to accept the fact that I was not going to buy they would cease their importuning and look at me for a long moment as though assessing my possible reactions to a different kind of approach—their tongues are reputed to be intimidating on occasion—and then they would flounce away with no more than an indignant rustle of petticoats—or it may have been pound notes.

The only tinkers on whom I came to bestow my custom were 'Tinkerloo' and 'Jinty'. Tinkerloo was a rollicking, robust character who came by ramshackle car to plead with us to buy bootlaces and polish, hair grips and hand cream and to give us devastating insights into the lives of itinerants generally. His appearances were infrequent and, in the hope of encouraging him to come regularly, I bought from him each time he came though his hair grips nearly always showed signs of rust and his hand cream was redolent of bad silage. I asked one of the tinkers once why Tinkerloo did not visit the village as habitually as the rest.

'Ach, him, mam! He's a terrible bad man for the drink, that one,' he told me, with perfidious unction. 'Three times last year and this year already he's been in hospital to be cured of his elephants.'

I was surprised. Tinkerloo had never struck me as being an alcoholic, but the last time I saw him he confirmed it himself, blinking the tears from his eyes.

'Aye, mam, it's true. And now they're after havin' me in jail for three months. Three months, mam, and that for doin' the right and proper thing.'

'How was that?' I asked him.

'Well y'see, mam. Whenever I see them pink elephants that you do see, comin' up at you out of the heather, or trees maybe where there's no trees, as I dare say you've heard, mam. Well then, I says to myself, I says, "It's time you done somethin', Joe," I says. So I gets into my car and I just drives myself off to hospital. It's what I've always done, mam, for years now, ever since the curse struck me as a lad.' His body sagged miserably. 'An' now they've stopped me from doin' it by sendin' me to jail for it. What am I to do now?' he demanded sorrowfully.

'You could get someone else to drive you to hospital,' I told him.

He stared at me stupidly. 'You don't understand, mam,' he explained patiently. 'I couldn't get nobody to come in a car with me when I'm in that state. Why, I believe I'm as wild as a bull.' The tears came afresh to his eyes and I had to buy half a dozen tubes of hand cream and hundreds of rusty hair grips before he was even moderately comforted.

Jinty, the other tinker who was certain of my patronage, was a wiry little woman of unbounded optimism. She had a wide gap-toothed smile and a nose that peeled so lavishly from sunburn that I swear it became a visible fraction of an inch smaller each year. I observed as much to her once.

'Ach, no, it's not the sun that's my trouble with my nose. No, no, it's my man.'

'Your man?'

'Yes, indeed. He's a bacon and eggs man y'see and travellin' as we are all the time I canna always get it for him. If he doesn't get his bacon and eggs in a mornin' then I gets my nose punched.' She sighed. 'It's the same with the tea. Tea, tea, tea, it is for him every few minutes of the day and if there's no tea in the pot then it's a bang on the nose for me again.'

I pressed upon her a packet of tea which she accepted with gummy gratefulness. I had no bacon and it was too early for the hens to have laid but I suggested she should call back later. I made a pot of tea and we sat in the sunshine drinking it. For the sake of Jinty's poor nose I suppose we ought to have gone inside but the chimney had been smoking so badly that the kitchen was barely habitable. I apologized to Jinty telling her that I had been trying to get someone for weeks to come and sweep the chimney but that so far everyone had proved to be very elusive.

'Sure my man will do that for you this evenin',' she offered briskly.

I simulated interest in the offer, not believing for an instant that anything would come of it. The tinkers are notoriously averse to manual work and anyway I doubted if people living most of their lives in tents or in lorries would know the mechanics of sweeping a chimney. It was quite a surprise therefore about four o'clock in the afternoon to be confronted by a fat, panting but very inoffensive-looking little man who wore a bright plaid shirt and who was already sweating in gorgeous Technicolor. He was accompanied by a youth whose figure looked as though some would-be boy scout had been practising knots with it. They had come, they announced, to 'sweep my chimperly' and they were in a hurry. Evidently it was to be swept in the traditional Bruach way, for the youth was carrying a large bouquet of heather and the man was clutching a boulder of suitable size. Fortunately, I had let the fire go out; I showed them the ladder and the rope which had been in readiness for weeks. They tied the boulder and the heather to the rope and then Jinty's man climbed apprehensively on to the roof. I rushed inside and hurriedly threw dust sheets over the furniture, watched by the youth, who had followed me in and who now stood so still that in the confusion I neatly draped him in a dust sheet too.

'What are you going to do?' I asked him.

'I'll be after catchin' the soot,' he replied lethargically.

'What in?'

He looked blank. 'A pail?' he mumbled.

I had only one pail and I didn't want it used for soot. The youth took off his cap and gazed inside it uncertainly. I ran to get a sack but I was too late. There was a rumbling, grating noise from the chimney as the stone was lowered down and simultaneously a great plump of soot fell into the stove and overflowed on to the floor.

'That'll be the better of that,' gloated the youth on whom the sight of the soot seemed to have an electrifying effect. He jerked himself outside and repeated the words to his confederate on the roof. There were some more rumbles and still more soot. The youth returned, paddled his way through the soot to the fireplace and pushed his head up the chimney. The voice, in miniature, of Jinty's man came down.

'He's sayin' the stone's after stickin' in the chimperly and I'll need to go up beside him on the roof to try will it come out,' he translated, and jerked away again outside. There were a few moments of silence before the stone again began banging ominously in the chimney, though there were now only occasional spatters of soot. I got a shovel and a cardboard box and prepared to clear up the mess, but I tripped over some obstacle among the soot, doubtless the tinker's cap, and sat down unexpectedly in the midst of it, banging my funny-bone on the door of the oven. I was still sitting there rubbing it when the voices began. Now although I have often heard the expression 'swear like a tinker', not until that moment had I the remotest conception of what it could mean. I thought I was inured to malediction but the language that came down my chimney as those two tinkers struggled with the stone was indeed a revelation. I could only wonder that it did not pulverize the stone. It was blistering! It was excoriating! I could have sat and listened to it for hours.

Eventually the stone was dislodged and when the two performers came down from the roof and presented themselves for payment I was glad to know that my blushes were masked by soot.

'That chimperly,' Jinty's man said confidentially, 'she's that coarse inside, mam, she'd be the better of a bit of blasting.'

I drew a deep and tremulous breath. 'Well,' I said reverently, 'you've done your best, haven't you?'

I put some eggs into a bag and handed them to him. 'Will you give these to your wife?' I asked.

'My wife?' he looked startled. 'Who would that be?'

'Why, Jinty, of course,' I said. 'You are Jinty's man, aren't you?'

'Is that so?' He turned and spat reflectively. 'Indeed I got a good son from her right enough.' He waddled away contentedly, the youth dragging behind.

Sheena dropped in to see how I was getting on.

'I hear you had the tinks sweeping your chimbley,' she said. 'Did they make a good job of it?'

'I've yet to see,' I replied as I put a match to the paper and sticks. The stove had always been a depressingly sluggish burner. In the mornings when I got up I would light it and it would go out. I would light it again; it would show a little promise and then peter out. Oh, well, I would think to myself, third time lucky—and sometimes it was, but daily it had grown more temperamental so that lighting it had become more like the ritual of plucking petals from a daisy and saying 'he loves me, he loves me not'. This time the paper caught quickly; the sticks were soon crackling and the flames curling round the peats and spearing up the chimney. It was wonderful.

'I don't believe I've ever seen that fire burn so well as that before, even when Hamish and Mary had it,' exclaimed Sheena. 'My, but they must have given it a good cleanin'.'

'I think they very nearly cauterized it,' I murmured with a faint smile.

Sheena had come to tell me that she was due to attend the local hospital the following morning for an ear examination and she wanted me to look out for a tinker called 'Buggy Duck' from whom she was in the habit of buying most of Peter's clothing. He was expected to be in the village the next day and I was to buy socks, shirts, overalls and handkerchiefs for Peter. There was no bargaining to be done, she assured me, Buggy Duck always named a fair price.

Next morning when a huge, savage-looking man with great tussocky eyebrows and broken black teeth bared in a wide grin presented himself at my cottage I recognized him as 'Buggy Duck'. His great arms, bare to the elbow, were shaggy as autumn grass; the skin of his face resembled crusty brown bread. When I had first encountered Buggy Duck a year or so previously his appearance had terrified me—until he spoke. Like so many vast men his voice came out of his body like the squeak from a stuffed toy and every bit of his energy seemed to be concentrated on producing even that ludicrous falsetto. Today he had a little girl trotting beside him—his daughter possibly, but after my recent blunder I decided it was better to refrain from enquiring into tinker relationships, for it seems that some of them cannot endure the stigma of marriage. I led them into the kitchen and while Buggy Duck untied the brightly coloured cloth of his bundle the little girl sat munching concurrently cake and apple and sweets which she had collected from child-loving Bruachites. I picked up a pair of men's socks from the top of the pile and examined them. In a second Buggy Duck had whipped off his battered shoe and, balancing on one leg, was holding up his foot for my inspection.

'Goot, goot socks, these, mam. The same as I have on myself. A fortnight now I've been wearin' these and they chust dhrinks up the shweat.' His squeak was emphatically Highland. My nose corroborated his statement; I put aside half a dozen pairs.

'Those shirts,' I mused. 'I'm not at all sure of the size.' Mentally I was trying to compare the width of Peter's shoulders to those of Buggy Duck. I gasped as, with a swift convulsive movement of his body, Buggy Duck divested himself of his thick pullover and stood before me in shirt-sleeves.

'Same as I have on myself, mam. Try him across my shoulders for size,' he invited.

I measured hastily and put aside two shirts.

'Vests or combinations, mam?'

'No,' I said emphatically, and hurriedly pulled two pairs of overalls from his bundle, adding them to the shirts and socks.

'Handkerchiefs?'

I breathed again. He displayed his stock of handker-chiefs—a frenzy of polka-dotted pinks, fungus greens and passionate purples. I chose some of the least offensive, and asked him the prices of everything.

'That comes to an awful lot of money for those few things,' I said when he told me.

'Indeed, but the price of things these days makes one shiver,' he agreed passionately. With a gusty sigh he collapsed into a chair, taking the tea I proffered and sucking it into his mouth noisily.

I turned my attention to the child. She was wet-nosed, sticky-lipped and carelessly dressed, but her hair was the colour of sun on corn stubble and her eyes had been put in with an inky finger. Her name, Buggy Duck told me, was Euphemia, 'Phimmy' for short. Normally tinker children are too reticent to speak to anyone, but this child answered me pertly when I asked how old she was.

'Five.' She stared around the room, missing nothing it seemed. 'You have six elephants, so you have,' she accused as her eye lighted on the parade of ebony elephants strung out along the mantelpiece.

'So I have.'

'You have seventeen books on that shelf, so you have.'

'That's right.'

'I think you must like elephants and books, so you must.'

'I think,' I said, 'that you are a very clever little girl, Phimmy, to be able to count up to seventeen when you're only five years old.'

'So I am,' she agreed complacently.

Buggy Duck reached for my cup and tilted it critically. 'Oh, to be sure, mam, there's happiness in store for you.' The purchase of socks, shirts, overalls and handkerchiefs, I felt, ought certainly to have ensured an auspicious future.

'Go on,' I encouraged.

'You're goin' to come into some money,' he predicted

with shrill earnestness.

'I'll need to if I'm going to buy from you,' I countered.

He snorted: a magnificent sound which embodied all the resonance his voice lacked. He stood up and began tying his bundle.

'Well, mam, my thanks to you and good luck till next year.' (Just like a tinker to wish good luck by instalments.)

I walked down the path beside them. Phimmy rushed ahead through the gate. The child interested me and I wanted to impress upon Buggy Duck that she was an exceedingly bright child, and to plead that her education should not be the haphazard thing it is with most tinker children.

'Phimmy,' I began seriously, 'is an exceptionally intelligent little girl.'

'Oh, so she should be, mam,' he agreed eagerly; 'it was a doctor himself who fathered her.'

Phimmy ran back to us. 'There's a bag with his pipes coming up the road,' she burst out excitedly.

I was on the point of correcting her when I saw the shape of the piper and decided it was not really necessary.

'He's getting the wind up now,' she announced. 'He's going to play.'

The piper turned in at the gate. I like the bagpipes moderately, though I think the fitting of suppressors should be made compulsory. At a reasonable distance they provide the ideal music for the country of hill and glen, surging and wailing as it does. The trouble is that their devotees seem to think that six feet from one's ears is a reasonable distance and more than once I have had to suffer the torment of being entertained by a piper blowing at full blast within the confined space of a bus.

Phimmy danced and jigged. Buggy Duck tapped his foot and nodded his head. I fixed a perfidious smile on my face and endured. My spirits rose as a black cloud, no bigger than a child could hold in its fist, brought a swift sharp shower, but we only shuffled back to the shelter of the cottage and the piper did not cease for the space of a breath. Indoors the noise was shattering and I recalled Jinty's man's advice regarding the chimney. It was getting a blast now all right.

At last the performance droned away to silence and Buggy Duck and Phimmy departed; the piper waited expectantly until I pressed a coin into his hand when a smile that was as thick and dirty as a swipe of tar parted his lips. 'My thanks, mam,' he muttered sepulchrally.

With the onset of autumn the tinkers gradually deserted us, leaving behind them the traces of their fires by the roadside and discarded shoes, garments and broken utensils littering the heather.

'I believe we're seein' tse last of tsem for tsis year,' said Hector, as we watched a number of them climbing wearily on to their lorry one rainy day.

'Good riddance too,' said Erchy feelingly. 'You remember that last lot was here a week ago? Got their lorry stuck in the ditch they did and they sent word for some of us to go and try would we get it out. A few of us went right enough, me and Hector was two of them, and by God! we'd no sooner got their lorry back on to the road than they was pulling out their bundles and trying to sell us shirts and socks and things, right, left and centre. Out there, mind you, beside the road! Indeed I believe they put their lorry in the ditch on purpose just to get us there.'

I was startled the next morning when I drew back my curtains to see a perambulator at the bottom of my garden. I stared at it, unable to believe my eyes. I was sure there had never been a perambulator in Bruach. No baby would have survived being pushed over roads like ours. I went to investigate, circling it as a suspicious animal circles bait. It was certainly a perambulator—not a new one but in quite good condition. I simply could not account for its presence there and the only thing to do was to wait and see what happened. Nothing did happen, so I went to see Morag.

'Morag,' I said, feeling very, very foolish indeed. 'There's a perambulator at the bottom of my garden.'

'Is there now?' she asked with indulgent surprise.

'Who put it there?' I demanded.

'Was it not yourself put it there?'

'Of course not,' I repudiated indignantly. 'How could I?'

'Indeed I don't know then. You'd best ask Erchy.'

I found Erchy mucking out his cow byre.

'Erchy,' I said, 'there's a perambulator at the bottom of my garden. Can you tell me why?'

'Nothin' to do with me,' he disclaimed with virtuous alacrity.

'Has anyone put it there for a joke?' I persisted.

'There's never been a perambulator in the village that

I've ever seen so how could they?' he asked.

'I can't understand it,' I said.

Erchy thought for a moment. 'It must have been them tinks left it,' he suggested.

We could think of no reason why the tinkers should bestow a permabulator on a middle-aged spinster.

'Oh, I mind now,' Erchy recalled. 'That last lot that was here when it was rainin'—they had a perambulator on the lorry and then they bought them old tanks from Murdoch. I dare say they hadn't room for everything so they'd just throw off the perambulator and your garden was as handy a place to leave it as anywhere. It's a wonder, though,' he added thoughtfully, 'that they didn't try to sell it to you.'

We decided that is what must have happened and no other explanation ever came to light.

'My, but you're lucky,' observed Erchy when someone referred to the subject a few days later.

'Lucky?' I echoed. 'Why?'

'You're lucky they only left you the perambulator. They might have left the baby in it too. You can never trust them tinks.'

VII. *Happy Band of Pilgrims?*

BRUACH SUFFERED FROM the misfortune of having no public hall and, though the education authorites were not averse to its use, some local demigod was always sure to raise objections if the school were suggested for any social function.

'We canna' even have that W.R.I. here,' Morag told me and Behag indignantly, 'just because some folks thinks it's too sexular.'

As a consequence the only communal relaxations for the crofters within the village were the church services on Sundays; the biannual communions; an election meeting once in five years and an even less frequent lecture by the poultry adviser, more familiarly known as the 'henwife'. During the winter months our evenings were sometimes enlivened by the visits of young lay preachers, locally termed 'pilgrims', who, with varying degrees of fanaticism, would exhort us poor sinners—who listened with varying degrees of perplexity—to forsake our evil ways and return to the paths of righteousness. Some of the pilgrims stayed for as long as a week amongst us and every night we would endure the hard benches of the church while they, with white strained faces, tear-filled eyes and voices that not only grated with emotion but also implied chronic deafness of the congregation if not of the Almighty, besought for us forgiveness and salvation. Mouthing the name of the Diety with expletive violence they would adjure us to give up our pipe-smoking, our church socials and our concubines. (Curiously enough I never heard alcoholism specifically mentioned as a sin but I suppose even the most zealous of pilgrims must recognize the hopelessness of some tasks.)

'What's a concubine?' Erchy asked, after one such meeting.

'It's a woman a man takes to live with him but who isn't his wife,' I explained.

'A mistress, like?'

'Yes.'

'Indeed we don't do that sort of thing hereabouts,' refuted Erchy. 'Why would we take them to live with us when they have homes of their own already?'

But, at a ceilidh a few weeks later at Morag's house, Erchy referred again to the subject of concubinage.

'I didn't think when those pilgrims was here that I knew of anybody hereabouts that was livin' with a woman who wasn't his wife, but I remembered afterwards about Dodo.'

'He's no from Bruach,' someone contradicted.

'No, I know fine he's not, but he was livin' with a

woman, right enough. And what's more he's had three children by her.'

'That fellow!' ejaculated Morag with righteous scorn.

Dodo was a shiftless, happy-go-lucky, slow-witted character who lived in a nearby village. His house was patchily cement-washed and his croft work was never quite finished because he was for ever neglecting it to start on some new job which in its turn was dropped before completion because some other project had taken his fancy.

'Well,' went on Erchy, 'when the pilgrims left here they went on to Dodo's place and they must have got a good hold of Dodo for I'm hearin' now that he and that woman slipped off quietly to Glasgow and he's married her.'

'Married her? After all these years?' we all echoed incredulously.

'Aye, that's what I'm hearin' and I believe it's the truth.'

There was a moment of silence as everyone digested the news and then Morag said, philosophically: 'Well, if he has, it's the first time I've ever known that man finish a job once he'd begun it.'

Because of the attention of the pilgrims it must not be supposed that the inhabitants of Bruach were any more godly or ungodly than any other community either in the Islands or elsewhere. It was certainly not to Bruach that a certain missionary was referring when he complained from the pulpit: 'The birds and the beasts and the roots of the the earth have their season, but the women of this place are always in season.' The village had never aspired to a church social—there was nowhere to hold such a function;

the practice of concubinage was, as Erchy had pointed out, rare enough to be discounted entirely; admittedly the pipe-smokers unregenerately smoked their pipes with as much pleasure when the pilgrims had departed as they had before they arrived. Nevertheless every pilgrim visiting Bruach could be sure of a full and ostensibly receptive congregation, for the innate courtesy of the Bruachites compelled them to attend the meetings. The pilgrims, they reasoned, like the henwife, had taken the trouble to come to the village in order to help them. They might be no more interested in the destiny of their souls than they were in the destiny of their poultry but they flocked to the services with dispassionate regularity and listened with evident piety. After the service the women would murmur sanctimoniously to one another, 'My, but wasn't he a good preacher,' or, 'What a splendid sermon that was,' for they are easily carried away by the tritest of dramatic performances; but once away from the church one could discern that little glint of hope behind the eyes that one of them would venture some comically outrageous aside and so allow them to untense themselves with a little burst of laughter. After long residence among them I do not believe that Gaels are essentially religious. They have been constrained by Calvinism, but their readiness to shed the constraint when circumstances appear to offer an excuse is, for me, sufficient proof that they have not absorbed it. They can be insufferably pious; they can also be sickeningly blasphemous. I recall once pausing on the threshold of a house I

140

was about to enter while a devout old man read with slow reverence the nightly passage from the Bible to his wife. The lamplit ritual of the scene was most impressive until the old man, coming to the end of the reading, shut the Bible with a snap and, slinging it across the table towards his wife, commanded her to 'Put that bloody thing away now.' I remember too an irrepressible old bachelor living alone, who would no more have considered taking a bite of food without first asking the blessing on it than of paying his rates without first receiving the final demand note; after a stormy night which had stripped part of his roof so that the ensuing rain squalls sent dismal trickles down into his kitchen, he was sitting before a bowl of breakfast porridge, asking for the customary blessing. As he came to the end of his prayer a steady jet of water descended from the roof directly into his bowl. Unhurriedly he said the 'Amen' and then without noticeable pause or alteration of tone he went on, 'But beggin' your pardon, Lord, I'd thank you not to go pissin' in my porridge.'

So, with negligible effect on the community, the various religious representatives, all indifferently referred to as 'pilgrims', came and went. Once Bruach had been startled to find a black-robed priest in its midst; a kindly, jovial man who was every day to be seen striding the rough moors or climbing the hills, his black robes fluttering around him. 'Puttin' all the hens off their layin', that's all he does,' Morag grumbled to me.

Since I had come to live in Bruach a second church had

been built so that it was no longer necessary for the two sects to hold joint services.* The new church was about half a mile farther along the road than the old one and was similarly constructed of plain corrugated iron. It was to this new church that Morag, Behag, Kate and myself set out one Wednesday in October to hear the last of a series of services conducted by two earnest young men who were making an evangelistic tour of the Hebrides which, they hoped, would arrest if not recall the great number of people who had back-slidden since their previous visit. The opening of their campaign in Bruach had been accompanied by the onslaught of a fierce gale which had raged almost without respite throughout the first four or five days, buffeting the walls of the church and driving rain and leaden hail against the roof with machine-gun force. During the last day or two, however, the storm had moderated, first into busy squalls with flurries of hailstones that stung one's cheeks like hot sparks, then into frisky breezes that brought tinsel-like rain, and finally this evening into a dramatic calm that was intensified by the steady sibilance of the sea outside the bay. Above the decor of hill peaks the stars flicked on haphazardly and the immature moon peeped out from a stage-wing of cloud, like a too-impetuous performer.

A tall figure leading a cow on a rope loomed up before us as we approached the church.

'Surely you're no bringin' the cow to the service, Ruari?' shouted Morag.

'Service?' bawled deaf Ruari.

*See *The Hills Is Lonely.*

'Aye, at the church tonight,' replied Morag patiently. 'What are they after havin' the bull at the church for?' demanded Ruari. 'No wonder I canna' find him. Here's me been leadin' this beast round since twelve o'clock this mornin' and no a sign did I see of him yet. I was thinkin' he must have gone over a cliff. At the church indeed!' his tirade rumbled into disgusted expectoration.

Morag took hold of his ear and explained firmly. 'It's they privileges. They're holdin' a service again tonight. There's no bull at the church.'

'Here, here, but the bull was down in the Glen yesterday. I saw him myself. He can no be far away,' volunteered Kate.

'He could be far enough,' muttered Ruari, sitting down by the road and wiping his hand over his face. 'I'm tired out lookin' for him.'

'Then come and sit in the church and listen to the privileges,' suggested Morag. 'It's no use sittin' there on the wet grass where you'll get your death of cold.'

'It's too late to take her to the bull tonight,' said Kate. 'D'ye think she'll hold till mornin'?'

'She might,' admitted Ruari half-heartedly.

'Ach then, see and tie her to the post just and come to the service,' instructed Morag, taking the rope from the unresisting Ruari and tying it round a telegraph pole.

Obediently Ruari followed us into the church whither we were pursued by reproachful bawls from the cow. We were late, so we had to sit in the front row, the church having filled from the back. The pilgrims, with resolutely happy faces, were ready to start.

Several times during the week I had encountered the pilgrims on my daily walks and always it was difficult to reconcile the pleasant-spoken, normally intelligent young men with whom I conversed with the two who from the pulpit stridently harangued the congregation each evening. Tonight they seemed to be even more emotionally tense than hitherto. Taking their text from the Acts of the Apostles they warned us, contradicted by frustrated bawls from Ruari's cow, not to emulate Felix and 'await our more convenient season'. They illustrated the text by relating to us the story of a young man who had elected to postpone his decision on conversion until after he had attended a social function in the church hall. At this function the young man had caught a cold which had rapidly progressed to pneumonia and when at last he lay dying he had charged the evangelists to ensure that when his coffin was carried past the church hall they should stop and give the people this message: 'I am in everlasting damnation and all because of a social and dance in the church hall.' The pilgrim, the muscles of his face and throat working, paused for a full threatening minute to allow the congregation to reflect upon the tragedy. Ruari's cow did not pause for an instant, but bellowed despairingly. No one appeared to be much affected by either performance. 'Ah, my friends,' continued the pilgrim, battling manfully against an obvious desire to weep; 'that young man waited his more convenient season and it was too late.' At this juncture he was so overcome by emotion that he had to sit down hurriedly in the pulpit and cover his face with a handkerchief while his partner took over the rest of the service. We sang a hymn and after being adjured once again to get rid of any 'Drusillas in our midst' we paid our fee at the door and filed out.

'Well done!' was Morag's first remark and I, thinking she was commenting on the sermon, was about to agree spinelessly, when I saw her eyes were on the moonlit road in front of us.

Kate's guess that the bull could not be far away had apparently not been very wide of the mark and the bellowed invitations of the cow had brought him to her. 'She wasn't goin' to wait her more convenient season,' whispered Kate wickedly.

I was not at all surprised to hear the following morning that after the service the bus, packed with members of the congregation, had left Bruach for a dance in the next village. In the wee small hours, long after the exultant pilgrims had retired to their beds, they were blissfully unaware that the noise of engines that penetrated their celestial dreams announced the return of last night's congregation, or a significant part of it, exhausted after a fervid dancing session and not a little the worse for whisky. It was still later that Angus and Hector arrived home. They had taken their rifles with them in the bus and dropped off on the return journey so as to go poaching venison at first light.

The two male pilgrims were soon followed by two middle-aged lady pilgrims who, no doubt feeling that the Bruachites were in need of constant rather than intermittent ministration, moved into the empty house adjoining the burial ground and prepared for a lengthy stay. One was a spinster, tiny, shiny, plump and gushing, with small blue eyes which glistened with tears whenever she was emotionally aroused, as perhaps by an observation on the weather or by the receipt of a compliment on a pretty dress. The other was a widow who had been married briefly to a jockey. She was dark and morose, with curiously mottled cheeks which looked as though they might have been used for stubbing out cigarettes, and her long, thin face constantly wore such an outraged expression that it reminded me of an emphatic exclamation mark. Also she had a pronounced stammer and in no time at all the village had dubbed them 'Flutter and Stutter'. They did not, I think, belong to any particular denomination and from Stutter's faintly servile attitude one got the impression that her religion was a very neutral affair, whipped into fervour only when necessary to appease her more ecstatic companion and so ensure a continuance of her favours. Flutter's religion was, I am convinced, mainly glandular.

When she was not occupied with religious meetings or in visiting, Flutter knitted prolifically and was distressed because she could find no market for her work. Stutter's quaint hobby was the making of finger-stalls from odd scraps of material; checked ginghams, pyjama cloth, tartan, all were neatly sewn and finished with white tape. I ordered one of Flutter's jerseys, which made her so happy the tears spilled over. I could have cried too when I got the jersey home and found it would have amply made a loose cover for my armchair.

Fortunately, Stutter did not try to sell her finger-stalls but she generously left me a bundle of them whenever she visited me. After she had gone I used to examine my fingers critically, counting them to make sure I really had only ten, and then I would count again the rising stock of finger-stalls in my first-aid tin which at its peak totalled a hundred and six.

Because they were female 'privileges' and because they preached happiness instead of hell-fire, the men did not feel it incumbent on them to attend the weekly meetings which the two pilgrims held in their cottage, but the women, with their more pliable conscience and glad of any diversion, turned up regularly to sing hymns and be read to by Flutter. Sometimes the readings were from the Bible but just as often they were stories from missionary magazines or, on particularly exciting evenings, from *The Man-Eaters of Kumaan* or even *King Solomon's Mines*. For the reading Miss Flutter invariably took up her position directly in front of a mirror above the fireplace into which she glanced frequently for reassurance. When it was time for prayers, regardless of the work-a-day attire of her congregation, she would take her hat from the dresser and carefully arrange it on her head before announcing 'We will now try to put up a little prayer,' much in the same way as a poacher might confide that he was going to 'try to put up a little grouse'. I must admit there were times when the 'Go-back, go-back' cry of the disturbed grouse would have seemed an appropriate response. These meetings were repeated on Sundays for the children of those parents prepared to endure the jeremiad tongues and lashing sarcasm of their Calvinistic elders to whom Sunday school was frivolous to the point of profanity. At the Sunday meetings and to a semblance of the tune of 'Hear the Pennies Dropping' extracted from a tortured violin by Miss Stutter, the children were invited to drop their pennies into a 'Present from Blackpool' teapot. In return they received a gaily coloured tract card; when the pilgrims ran out of tract cards they substituted cigarette cards. The children thought little of Flutter's reading; they thought even less of Stutter's violin ('It's as wicked as the bagpipes on a Sunday but it's no half as good a noise,' one little boy confided to me); some of them reckoned a coloured card a very poor return for their penny, yet, because it was somewhere to go to escape the smothering Sabbath piety of their own homes, the children attended with a regularity that both flattered and astonished the pilgrims. So much so that they decided to give a party as a reward, some of the money they had collected being used to provide the refreshments. Now although many of the crofters had been broad-minded enough to join in the services at the cottage the association of parties with religion was to them completely unacceptable and though it was only obliquely expressed the pilgrims would not have needed undue powers of perception to have become aware of the general disapproval of their project but, happily insulated by their own egotism, they sailed along with the arrangements. Miss Flutter resolutely learned poetry to recite. Miss Stutter practised her violin, while both made the rounds of the village extracting so many faithful promises of attendance that I wondered what the outcome of it all would be.

On the day and at the time stated I set out for 'Pilgrim Cottage' expecting to meet up with others along the road. Sarah called to me from the door of her own cottage.

'Aren't you coming to the party?' I asked, seeing that she was still wearing gumboots and old clothes.

'Indeed no, my dear. The cow's just near calvin' and I canna' leave him now.'

'I can see to him myself,' interpolated her brother, who was carrying a pail of water into the house. 'You can go to the party, right enough.'

'Ach well, d'you see, I canna' find one of my stockings,' Sarah went on glibly. 'I had it for church last Sunday, and I dare say I threw it under the bed the same as I always do, but where it is now nobody can say.'

I could offer no help as Sarah wore only thick black woollen stockings. Not long after I had said good-bye to her with the promise that I would convey her apologies to the pilgrims, the bus pulled up alongside me.

'Are you comin' to the fillums?' Johnny, the driver, asked.

'No, I'm going to the party,' I replied. 'Aren't you coming?'

'Well we were thinkin' of it right enough.' He turned for confirmation to the dozen or so passengers he was carrying. 'But you see it's *Whisky Galore* they're showin' and we might never get a chance to see it if we don't go tonight.'

'I'll have to go to the party,' I said. 'I did promise faith-fully I'd go.'

'Didn't we all,' said Johnny lightly and everyone laughed as the bus started off again.

The Bruach road was busy. Hector, whom I had heard swear to cut his throat and wish to die if he didn't attend the party, was now coming towards me, pushing a bicycle. I asked him whether he was coming.

'Ach no, my cycle's broke and I'm away to Padruig's to see has he got a tsing will mend it.'

It looked as though attendance at the party was going to be sparse indeed. Morag had butter to churn and the cream would not keep until morning and Fiona had been sick all day, so neither she nor Behag could come.

When I reached the cottage I was greeted by the flus-tered and delighted pilgrims. Miss Flutter was dabbing con-tinually at her brimming eyes; Miss Stutter was wearing exotic finger-stalls on two fingers of her left hand. Inside, I was confronted by a large table bearing innumerable plates each piled high with sandwiches of a variety of pallid-looking fillings. Miss Flutter began to introduce me to each plate-ful; egg and cheese; cheese and egg; cheese; egg; meat paste; fish. When she was unsure of a filling she lifted the lid of a sandwich and peered.

We sat down to await the rest of the guests, I with steadily increasing dismay. When the kettles on the side of the stove had been sighing for nearly two hours and the tops of the sandwiches were beginning to curl querulously, Miss Stutter decided that she had better make the tea.

'I've made it nice and strong, so that we can add plenty of water to it when they come,' she said with tenacious optimism as she poured me a cup that was the colour of faded sun tan. Miss Flutter, by now completely dry-eyed, invited me to try a sandwich. I chose a salmon filling; she looked puzzled.

'I haven't any salmon,' she said.

'Oh, I beg your pardon,' I apolgized. 'I heard you say fish and as it looked pink I took it to be salmon.'

'Oh, no, this is cod,' she corrected me with an earnest smile and handed me the plate. 'It's a recipe we invented ourselves to use up some that was left over.' She took a closer look at the plate. 'But they've turned pink!' She stared accusingly at Miss Stutter, who looked guiltily down at her two finger-stalls and then surreptitiously put her hand behind her back. I changed my mind and had cheese.

When ten o'clock came round and still no one but myself had arrived for the party, the despondent pilgrims packed away the sandwiches into tins. I hoped that this might mean I could escape but they felt that as I had taken the trouble to come I must be entertained, and so I sat submissively while Miss Flutter rendered *The Lady of Shallott*, *The Forsaken Merman* and *Abou Ben Adhem*, and Miss Stutter chafed her violin with its bow and elicited from it jig-like noises that were no more musical than a two-stroke engine.

The following day the Bruachites were abject in their excuses and apologies to the pilgrims and made such asseverations of their disappointment at missing the party that the pilgrims were ready to believe the fiasco had been largely due to their own mismanagement.

'You know,' said Erchy, when he strolled into my kitchen some days later; 'Hamish had to take a gas cylinder to those pilgrims yesterday and he says they're still eatin' their way through piles of stale sandwiches. They asked him to stay for tea, but he knew fine what he was in for, so he said he had to go to the hill. They've asked quite a few in to tea since the party, but everybody's too wise to go.'

'It really was too bad,' I told him. 'They did ask everyone first and nearly everyone said they would go.'

'What else can you say when people asks you straight out like that?' he demanded. 'You can't just tell them you won't go.'

'Why not?'

'They'll want to know then why you won't go, and if you give them a reason like as not it will turn out to be a lie. It's easier to tell them yes.' He sat down by the window and lit a cigarette.

'How did you like *Whisky Galore*?' I asked him.

'It was grand,' he replied. 'My but they got drunk there, I'm tellin' you.'

'Drunker than people get here?' I asked doubtfully.

He pondered my question for a moment. 'Well,' he conceded, 'it looked to me as if they was pretty drunk, but what I couldn't understand is, they was in their ordinary working clothes. Ach, I don't think they can have been drunk at all or they would have had on their best clothes. I think they was only acting.'

Erchy had dropped in on me on his way back from gathering hazels for a lobster creel he was making for me. I had bought a small, light dinghy, one that I could launch and pull up the beach unaided, and Erchy, knowing my fondness for lobsters, had suggested that I put out a creel and try catching them for myself. It was now my ambition to sit down to a meal of fish I had caught; bread and butter I had made; vegetables and fruit I had grown; so the prospect of a lobster creel pleased me as much as the prospect of a bottle of French perfume would have a few years before.

'What are you makin' now?' Erchy asked, as he watched me breaking eggs—from my own hens—into a bowl.

'Lemon curd,' I replied.

'Now that's stuff I like,' he enthused. 'There's only one thing I like better and that's blackcurrant jam.'

'I like blackcurrant jam too,' I admitted sorrowfully. The garden of the cottage had been a tatter of blackcurrant bushes when I took over and I had cut them all down to ground level. Since then they had yielded seven blackcurrants.

'I'll get you plenty blackcurrants if you'll make them into jam,' Erchy offered.

'I'll make them into jam quickly enough,' I agreed. 'But where are you going to get blackcurrants?'

'Never you mind,' said Erchy. 'You provide the sugar and I'll provide the blackcurrants and we'll split fifty-fifty.'

Though Erchy's mother was an excellent baker of girdle scones and bannocks she had never tried her hand at making jam and was completely confident that she could never achieve a 'jell'. Indeed, few of the crofters made any attempt at jam-making despite the abundance of blackberries and brambles in their season. Those with families had no storage space; and the women complained that if they did make half a dozen jars of jam then each member of the family would take a jar and a spoon and eat the whole lot at one sitting. So I agreed to Erchy's proposal.

The following Thursday evening I went along to 'Pilgrim Cottage' for the weekly meeting. It seemed as though the villagers, ashamed of their absence from the pilgrim's party, were trying to make up for it by their attendance tonight. The women and children crowded the little cottage and we had to have the door open so that the menfolk standing outside could join in. Erchy, Johnny, Hector, Alistair, Angus, all were there. Miss Flutter was ecstatic; she lost her place when reading several times, and put her hat on back to front for the prayers. The hymns were sung so lustily that Miss Stutter's violin could be heard only for a bar or two when it managed to get away ahead of the rest of the starters. When the meeting closed the two radiant pilgrims waved blessings and good-byes from the doorstep until we were out of hearing. My own feelings of vexation at the behaviour of the Bruachites towards the pilgrims the previous week melted. It seemed that they felt genuine compunction for their neglect, and when, the following morning, Erchy brought the promised blackcurrants—two milk pails full—I mentioned to him how much pleasure it had given the pilgrims to see such a good turn-out. He agreed with me abruptly and left.

There were about ten pounds of blackcurrants and I had eight full jars on the table ready for labelling and another panful of jam boiling on the stove when Miss Flutter called.

'Oh, you're making jam,' she observed. 'Blackcurrant too,' she sniffed appreciatively. 'You know, we thought we'd make blackcurrant jam today too. We had such a lovely lot of blackcurrants on our bushes only yesterday afternoon, but we decided to leave them until today.' She sighed. 'Now we're wishing we'd picked them because when we went out to get them this morning there wasn't one to be seen. Could the birds have stripped them so quickly, do you think?'

I was quite certain they couldn't have. I was ready for Erchy when he called to collect his jam later that evening.

'Erchy, where did you get those blackcurrants?'

'From the pilgrims' cottage. Where else?'

'When?'

'When we was at the meeting last night. Why else do you think we went there? All us boys had to go, some to do the pickin' and some to do the singin'. When they sang very loud it was to warn us that one of the pilgrims was near the door and we'd need to dodge back to the service. Ach, what are you worryin' about? They would have been wasted if we hadn't got them.'

'They were going to make jam themselves today,' I told him. 'Miss Flutter was here this afternoon and told me that when they came to pick the blackcurrants they'd all gone.'

'She only wants things after she can't have them,' Erchy retorted.

'I feel terrible about it,' I said miserably.

'Ach, just you give her a pot of jam and shut her up,' he soothed. 'Aye, and give her one from me too. That'll be more jam than ever she would have got from her blackcurrants.'

Miss Flutter and Miss Stutter were very very grateful for the two jars of jam. They no doubt used it to help down the last of the sandwiches.

VIII. *Back to School*

THE GREAT TIT IN the rowan tree behind the house had been calling 'tea-cher, tea-cher' since early morning. I little thought at the time that he was being prophetic but, later in the afternoon when I was gathering an armful of washing from the line, I turned to see the head teacher of the school striding towards me. When I had first come to Bruach with its scattered houses and discovered its preponderance of spinsters, bachelors and old-age pensioners, I had been a little surprised to find that there was a village school.

'But are there any children to attend it?' I had asked artlessly.

'Surely, we can make children here the same as they do everywhere else, you know,' Erchy had retorted with ruthless indelicacy.

The heavy figure of the head teacher leaned over me as she spoke with pious sibilance. It seemed that Elspeth, the junior teacher, had been taken ill suddenly and would not be able to carry out her duties for a few days. The head herself was suffering from a severe cold and was finding the strain of double duty a little too much. Would I, she pleaded, step into the breach temporarily? I liked the idea, particularly as Mary, my friend from England, was due to arrive the following day to stay with me and I knew she would be delighted to have Bonny and the chickens to minister to for a little while.

The Bruach school consisted of one classroom divided by a green baize curtain with about ten double desks on either side. When I entered the first morning the head teacher was already there. She introduced me briefly to the work in hand and gave me instructions, and while we awaited the arrival of the children we conversed together with the taut heartiness of two women who have little in common.

'I hope you don't object to my washing,' she hissed, indicating a pan of sheets that was bubbling away on the side of the fire; 'but with not being so well lately I've got behind myself with everything.'

At ten o'clock the children filed in, their eyes fixed on me with passionate interest. Johnny, who had given me my first lesson in fishing from the rocks, was there among the bigger boys, and the twins, whom I had long ago christened 'Giggle and Sniggle', each a complete replica of the other, were huddled into a desk together, bringing with them a lingering atmosphere of the ceilidhs. When the children were settled the head read the morning prayer and the whole school recited the Lord's Prayer in measured tones, their rich highland voices lingering on the r's and softening the consonants. I noticed they rendered the third line of the prayer as 'Thou will be done on earth' and thought irreverently that from what I had seen of the behaviour of some of the little scamps out of school hours the substitution of the personal pronoun for the possessive was not inapt.

I took out the register.

Once in Bruach I had been approached by a stranger and asked if I could direct him to the house of a Mr. McAnon. Out of a total population of a little over two hundred, it had been necessary to explain to him, there were fifteen Mr. McAnons. It was Mr. Lachlan McAnon he wanted. The information made identification only a little easier, there being five Lachlan McAnons. I probed for other details. Was the Mr. McAnon married? Yes, in his letter he had referred to a wife. The number of possibilities was cut to three. Was he dark or red-haired? He didn't know, but if it would be of any help he could show me a sample of handwriting. I doubted it; I had been struck by the fact that all Bruachites seemed to have similar handwriting. Some might be more literate than the rest but they all wrote with the same painstaking legibility and added identical flourishes. A graphologist would probably have judged them to be of uniform character. However, by a process of elimination we did at last manage to select a suitable Mr. McAnon for him to call upon and it transpired that it was the right one.

The calling of the register was much like my experience with the stranger, the majority of the children bearing the same clan surname and, because the custom of naming children after relatives was followed slavishly, there being much duplication of Christian names. In my small class I found I had two Alistairs; two Angus's; three Floras; and two Morags. Two of the Floras were sisters, the elder being named for her mother and known as 'FloraVor' (Big Flora) and the younger being named for her grandmother and known as 'FloraVic' (Little Flora). It was fortunate that I knew them all by sight.

My class struggled over their arithmetic, muttering, coughing, scratching their heads, jabbing pens into inkwells and doing all the other things that children do in a classroom. Fiona lifted her head and stared at me coolly. She disliked school and tended to be rebellious in class. Giggle and Sniggle, their hair-styles making them look as though they were going to take wing at any moment, chewed pens and whispered to each other. Both twins were backward, hence their presence in the junior class. A series of sniffs, resonant with satisfaction, claimed my attention and I traced them to a little boy with an exceedingly turned-up nose whom I knew only as 'Beag a Mor' (Big and Small). Apparently he had been given the same name as an elder brother and when the brother had died the younger one, for some implausible reason, had inherited both adjectives. I went over and asked him quietly if he had a handkerchief. He delved into a pocket and after much rummaging produced a filthy tatter that led me to suspect that his nose might have turned up at the sight of it. Seeing my look of revulsion he explained engagingly that his handkerchief was not dirty. It was just that it had been tucked under a black jersey he had been wearing and when the jersey had got wet it had leaked.

As the children worked, there arose a strong tang of seaweed that competed with the smell of soapy washing to fill the classroom. Most of them were chewing and when they thought my attention was elsewhere they would furtively pull from under their desks sections of the peeled stalks of tangle-wrack, which they called 'staff', and from which they took large bites.

From the other side of the curtain came the sibilant voice of the head teacher who was putting her class through the agonies of mental arithmetic.

'If one egg costs twopence halfpenny, how much does twelve eggs cost?' and without waiting for an answer she carried on conversationally, 'Did your mother's hens lay yet, Jessac?'

'No, they didn't yet.'

'Fancy that! I got eight from my fifteen yesterday. Did yours lay, Johnny?' Johnny's reply was inaudible. 'See and tell your mother to put in some spice with their food. The van sells it and it makes a great difference, I find. Now where were we?'

After a few more questions asked and answered her voice again penetrated my consciousness.

'If ten pounds of sultanas . . . Annac, did I not hear

your mother askin' at the van for sultanas last week?'

'I believe she did.'

'Well, mind and tell her when you get home that Ian the shop has some lovely ones, but she'll need to hurry because everybody was buying them to make dumplings when I was there.'

And again: 'Pomegranates are threepence halfpenny. . . . Has anyone here seen a pomegranate?' No one had apparently because she went on to explain ingenuously: 'It's a fruit like a cucumber. Anyone who's seen a cucumber has very nearly seen a pomegranate.'

When written arithmetic was substituted for mental she set them the old faithful one of the taps and the water cistern but adroitly she rendered it, 'If your boat was leaking and the sea was comin' into it. . . .'

Thus companionably lessons progressed. Was it perhaps, I mused, partly because of homely observations such as these that Highland education is second to none? My musings were interrupted by a knock on the door of the classroom and the teacher, answering it, stayed talking to someone in the porch for a few minutes.

'It's the shepherd,' she came through the curtain and whispered to me hoarsely. 'He's after leavin' his job here and he's wantin' me to write him a reference.'

When morning break came the head took her pan of sheets and prevailed upon the canteen cook to give her a hand with the wringing and before the end of break they were billowing on the line across the school garden. At lunch time the children trooped into the tiny canteen shed at the back of the school where Giggle and Sniggle were deputed to act as waitresses. There were so many eager hands ready to grasp the plates as they appeared, however, that serving was accomplished with astonishing rapidity, as indeed was everything else. The meal began with Scotch broth and uproar.

'Anyone want my vegetables?' shouted the teacher as she ladled up her soup and pushed the vegetables to the side of her plate. 'Big and Small' came over and claimed the barley but he did not want the vegetables. She repeated the question, standing up and offering her plate like a market woman offers a bargain: there were no takers. The speed with which the children shovelled down all their food was phenomenal. With grubby fingers they crammed the utensils into their mouths and gulped, spilled, gurgled and sucked like starved puppies. I watched them, spellbound, reflecting upon all the sore stomachs in Bruach and remembering that a tin of bicarbonate of soda was as much of a necessity on the table at mealtimes as sugar or salt and as familiar an ornament on a mantelpiece as a tea caddy.

'It's no wonder the canteen's full of rats,' said the teacher through a mouthful of mince; 'they spill that much of their food. I've had to get some rat poison and I'm goin' to put it down when school's over.' I offered to stay and help.

Giggle, leaning over me, whispered something that seemed to imply I was a 'cursed tart' but which I knew was merely an offer of custard with my prunes. The meal was cleared away while the cheeks of the children were still bulging with their last mouthfuls and we stood up and thanked God for what we had received, though I considered a more appropriate grace would have been 'Thank God we didn't choke'.

Outside the sun was brilliant, raining silver darts on the blue water and gilding the steep cliffs of the cove that sheltered the school. I sat on the steps watching the children, and the teacher brought out a basket of darning and joined me. There were few games the children could play in Bruach. It was nearly always too windy to skip; it was too steep for ball games; too rough for playing hop-scotch. The younger ones strolled now in groups along the shore, poking into rock pools or playing a clumsy game of 'tag' over the boulders. One child walked alone playing with a chopped-off hen's leg of which he pulled the exposed sinews so that the toes opened and closed with horrid agility. Some of the older boys had found a washed-up pit-prop and began a game of 'tossing the caber' while others played at 'fingerstones', a most peculiar game resembling rubbing one's tummy with one hand and patting one's head with the other. The first and second fingers of the left hand are slid to and fro over a boulder whilst the boulder is hit rhythmically with a stone held in the right hand. It is a savage method of I.Q. assessment, the less alert boys frequently hitting their fingers; it was considered a great joke locally to get the village idiot playing 'fingerstones'.

'You wouldn't like to go back to teaching?' asked the head suddenly.

'No, not at all.'

'Fancy! I wouldn't be without it. There's always somebody to talk to when you're teaching. Don't you ever get lonely?'

'How many of the children can swim?' I asked, deflecting her attention from myself.

'Why none of them, I don't believe.'

'It seems a pity, with the sea so close,' I said.

'More than a pity,' she agreed. 'Indeed the risks they take climbing about the rocks sometimes, I'd be a lot happier if they could swim.'

I said nothing but I thought I would talk over the matter with Mary, who was not only a splendid swimmer but was also a part-time swimming instructor.

When lessons began again the sun had moved round full on the schoolhouse windows. The fire had been left to go out but the classroom became increasingly torrid. The discarded chunks of staff under the desks became decidedly odiferous and the classroom began to give off the musty, sour smell of sweating children mingled with that of sunlight on dust-impregnated wood and cloth. The children were taking it in turns to read aloud from a book of fairy stories I had taken because there were none in the school library. I had to remind myself constantly that they were naturally Gaelic speakers with English only as an acquired language. Giggle's turn came at the end of the story and she faltered along, stabbing at the odd words she knew with expressionless indifference and shaping her mouth experimentally over the syllables of the rest. 'And . . . the . . . prin . . . cess . . . mar . . . married . . . the . . . d . . . duck. . . .' There was a burst of tittering from the class which I quelled with a look. I told her to read it through again but she still persisted on pronouncing 'duke' as 'duck'. Suppressed titters came again, this time not only from my own pupils but from the other side of the curtain where the class, with india rubbers audibly in evidence, were engaged in drawing a map of North Africa.

'Flora,' I reasoned with her, 'a princess wouldn't marry a duck, would she?' Flora stared at me with unblinking stupidity. I insisted she try again, telling her to use her common sense. It was of no avail. She was still determined to marry the princess to a duck.

Impatiently I turned to Sniggle, whose eyes were bright with contempt for her sister. 'Murdina,' I said, 'can you tell your sister what a princess would be likely to marry?'

Murdina's hand shot up eagerly. 'Yes, Miss. Please, Miss, it would have to be a drake.' The whole room dissolved into laughter and the teacher bustled from the other side of the curtain to add her ridicule before she called us firmly to attention for evening prayers.

I stayed behind when the children had gone, so that I could lend a hand with the rat poison and the teacher took the opportunity to show me the reference she had written out for the shepherd.

'Is he as good as this?' I asked doubtfully. It was an encomium. I doubt if there has ever been a better shepherd.

'You'll know him, of course?' she asked. 'He lives outside the village but he goes to my own church regularly.'

'I know that Netta had a baby by him a little while ago,' I admitted.

'Oh yes, indeed. But he's done the right thing by her. He's made sure the baby was registered under his own name.'

'But if he admits he's the father and wants the baby in his own name, why on earth didn't he marry the girl?'

The teacher looked at me in shocked surprise. 'Oh, Miss Peckwitt,' she hissed reproachfully, 'he's a good-living man and he's hoping to be a missionary some day. He could never marry a girl like that.'

We adjourned to the canteen and spread slices of bread with rat poison.

'They're supposed to become thirsty with this stuff and leave the premises in search of water and when they drink they die, isn't that the way it works?' I asked.

'Yes, but I think we'll make sure they can get at water here,' she said as she thoughtfully placed saucers of water in the cupboards.

'Have you used it before?' I asked her. 'Do you know how effective it is?'

'Well, I don't really, but Sandy Beag says it's good right enough.' She sniggered. 'Me and my husband were watching Sandy Beag put some rat poison down a few weeks ago round his sheds. I don't know if it was this stuff he was using then, but there he was carefully putting down pieces of baited bread and there at his heels was his dog following faithfully and eating every piece as it was laid down. Every now and then Sandy would catch him and swear at him and start laying the trail again, but he couldn't stop the dog. At last he shut the animal in the house, but it wasn't many minutes before it was out again and eating it. It was a good thing it wasn't harmful to domestic animals or Sandy would have lost the dog right enough, and he was fond of it.' She sniggered again. 'Indeed, I think he just decided he must put up with the rats after all.'

'He should try Erchy and Johnny's remedy,' I said, with a reminiscent smile. The story of how Erchy and Johnny had once been given the job of ridding an hotel outbuilding of rats had often been related in the village. The two rat catchers had stipulated that they be given a bottle of whisky apiece, their professed plan being to soak pieces of bread in the whisky and to wait until the rats got drunk on it. They would then pounce on the rats before they could dodge back to their holes and hit them on their heads. They swore that rats were attracted by whisky and that their method had proved effective several times previously. Armed with stout clubs the two of them reported for work one night and the hotel proprietor, sceptical but desperate, provided the whisky. But early the next morning, so the story goes, when he went to find out how the men had got on, he found Erchy and Johnny and several rats lying drunk on the floor—some of the rats being cradled in the crook of Erchy's arm. At his shout of rage the rats had sprung up and bolted unerringly for their holes, but the two apostates had managed to struggle to their feet only to collapse again under the full blast of his wrathful sarcasm. The most curious outcome of the night's affair was that, inexplicably, the rats thereafter deserted the outbuilding.

'Seein' the state those two were in was enough to drive

any self-respectin' rat away,' the hotel proprietor explained sardonically.

'It was your damty bad whisky that got rid of them,' retorted Erchy. 'And your damty bad language,' added Johnny morosely.

That evening I discussed with Mary the possibility of swimming lessons for the children. She fell in with the idea at once, and I sent a message to the mothers saying that any of the children who could bring a bathing suit and towel could stay after school if they wished to be given lessons— provided the weather remained calm and sunny. After break two or three of the scholars came to assure me that it was surely going to 'make a fine day'. They shook their cupped hands and opened them to show me horrid woodlice struggling on their backs. If the woodlice had rolled up into a ball it would have been a sure sign of rain.

The sun continued to shine, the wind stayed muzzled by the heat, and when school was over for the day every child was waiting on the shore.

'All right, go and get into your bathing suits,' I told them as Mary appeared. The girls flocked into the porch and the boys dove behind the playground walls and all emerged wearing their bathing suits—their ordinary wool vests with a large safety-pin between the legs. With Mary and me in attendance, they splashed through the strokes in the shallow water, the more promising ones being taken out individually and tutored in deeper water. When it was decided that they had had enough for the time being, they asked for a demonstration of swimming and Mary, who is as adept as a seal in the water, performed for her entranced audience willingly. Then she and I went into the schoolhouse for a 'strupak'. We were standing on the step taking our leave of the teacher when Seumas Beag, the father of the twins, came shuffling diffidently up to us.

'What are you wanting, Seumas?' the teacher teased him. 'Have you come to learn how to swim?'

'Not me indeed. I'll never learn to swim,' he replied.

'Why not? You're always out in boats. Wouldn't you feel better if you could swim?' I asked him.

'I would not. I was talkin' to a man who was drowned once and he warned me never to learn to swim. No, what I came for was the cailleach wanted me to tell you the twins is gettin' their tongues awful cut on the knives at the canteen. She's sayin' they're too sharp altogether.'

'It's their own fault entirely,' retorted the teacher loftily. 'They shouldn't push them so far into their mouths.'

'How do you manage to tell the twins apart?' I asked Seumas. 'I find it very difficult.'

'Indeed, some times I'm not knowin' that myself,' he admitted sadly. 'I was thinkin' I'd get the subsidy man to clip their ears for me the next time he comes same as he does with the calves.' A smile fumbled longingly at his lips.

'Why was Hamish not in school today Seumas?' the teacher taxed him.

'Ach, he's no well in himself,' replied Seumas shiftily.

'He was out on the hill last evening, I saw him myself. Was there anything wrong with him then?' she asked dryly.

'No, indeed. It was this mornin' just, after he'd taken his breakfast, he felt bad with a pain in his stomach.' Seumas started to shuffle hastily away.

'He'd probably eaten too much breakfast,' retorted the teacher.

'No more than two raw eggs boiled hard did he have,' contradicted Seumas indignantly as he hurried away.

'He's away to warn Hamish not to show himself,' commented the teacher knowingly. 'Indeed, the lice that man gives me is terrible.'

I knew from the puzzled expression on Mary's face that I should have to explain that the teacher was referring to Seumas's plausibility and not his parasites.

We decided that as the tide was low we would pick our way leisurely homeward along the beach and had not gone more than a few hundred yards when we came upon Sandy Beag himself with his gun and his dog, ensconced upon a rock looking out for likely 'skarts'. Sandy complimented Mary on her swimming, and then remarked that he thought we would soon have thunder.

'I was wonderin' if you'd teach my own dog here to swim,' he went on hopefully. 'Here's me after shootin' skarts day after day and the tide takin' them away on me because my dog cannot swim.'

'But all dogs can swim,' responded Mary, valiantly suppressing a smile.

'No this one, indeed,' argued Sandy Beag. 'I've thrown him in a couple of times and he's near drowned for fear of movin' his legs. I thought maybe if I took him out in my boat and threw him overboard and you'd be waitin' just by to grab him and wriggle his legs for him to see will he swim. If he knew that he should wriggle he'd maybe be all right after that.'

Mary laughingly refused to 'wriggle'. 'He's a nice dog,' she said, stroking the animal's head.

'Ach, he's nice enough, but he's no use to me at all. It's chasin' the hills myself I have to be while he just sits there watchin' me and scratchin' himself. Aye, but my wife is fond of him y'see so I canna get rid of him.' Thus he excused his own attachment to the dog.

Just at that moment Sandy jumped up, flung his cap in the air and flapped his sides with his arms. It is a contention of Bruach 'skart' shooters that if a 'skart' is swimming out of shooting range it will come close to investigate a cap thrown into the air, presumably believing it to be another 'skart'. The lure does appear to be effective.

'If I get this one I'll bring it round to you,' promised Sandy Beag.

Some people say that 'skarts' are not worth eating; that they taste fishy. In Bruach we buried them for three days and then we skinned them. There was not the slightest trace of fishiness about them after this treatment and the amount of meat on their breast and legs has to be seen to be believed. One boarding-house proprietor I know used to serve them up as 'sea turkey' and was often congratulated on the dish. Mary and I made a couple of very sleek and expensive-looking feather toques from their skins, simply by stretching them over a piece of pit-prop and then having them cured and lined.

After the heavy heat of the day I, at any rate, was tired and we sat long over tea watching a spider's web outside the window gradually filling with midges so that it began to resemble a faint pencil sketch being drawn over heavily with charcoal. The web had been there for some time for it was too perfect a thing to destroy. Each morning it had been cleaned of its catch and the spider grew perceptibly bigger and fatter. We wished him long life. I roused myself at last. It was the night for my fortnightly writing of Sarah's letters and Mary intended to stroll along with me and then go on up to the post office with her letters. Usually Sarah came over to the cottage with her writing materials but the hot weather had been very trying for her feet and I had promised tonight that I would go to her. Veiled against the midges we set out, Mary threatening to collect me on the way back so as to meet the fabulous Flora, who, though I had often described her in my letters, Mary maintained was too incredible for her to accept. To the south the sky was strangely lit and screened by still, dark clouds with deckled silver edges. The thunder Sandy had predicted murmured faintly behind the hills and the sea, sullen and shadowed, seemed to be growing chill with apprehension. The crofters we saw at work were rubbing the midges off their faces and necks.

Sarah had paper and envelopes already waiting for me and she appeared to be unusually flushed and excited.

'I want you to write to the Queen for me,' she blurted out as soon as I sat down at the table.

'The Queen,' I echoed, startled. 'What do you want to write to the Queen about, Sarah?'

'I want to write and ask her what she uses for her husband's corns,' she elucidated.

'But has the Duke of Edinburgh got corns?' I asked, vainly trying to recall some news item that might throw light on her resolve.

By way of explanation Sarah produced a recent photograph of the Duke of Edinburgh in polo kit. 'He must have corns,' she replied, pointing at his footwear. 'Wearin' they big boots would put corns on anybody's feets. You do as I say and write and ask her, mo ghaoil. She won't mind tellin' an old lady like myself who works hard and has such terrible feets, and she's bound to get the very best for him, you know.'

I have regretted ever since that I dissuaded Sarah from sending off that letter.

Mary called my name through the open door and came in to be staggered briefly by the impact of Flora, but there came a long drawn-out roll of thunder and big splodgy rain drops hit the stone steps so we cut short our visit and ran through the early dusk, now mercifully midge free, to the cottage. Mary sat by the window a little awe-struck by the sheer quantity of water that was sheeting down on to the sea and cascading from the shed roof to flay the full water-butts. I lit the lamp and started to mark the history books I had brought home from school. The class had been doing the battle of Mons Graupius and, perhaps because Elspeth would be returning to her duties in a day or two, I had taken special pains to ensure that they had a good grasp of the subject. They had written on the battle for homework and the first few books seemed to indicate that my toil had not been fruitless. I marked away happily. And then I opened Giggle's exercise book. My head flopped forward on to my hands as I stared in dismay at the solitary line of writing across the otherwise empty page: 'Mons Graupius was a big, fat man.' I read it again and again, puzzled by a vague consonance, and I groaned histrionically.

'What is it?' asked Mary, looking round. 'Goodness,' she went on, half rising from her seat, 'there's someone coming here, Becky. In this weather.'

'Anyone you know?' I asked indifferently.

'No, I don't think so, but I can't tell, he's all done up in oilskins. It's a man though. A big, fat man.'

'That,' I said heavily as I got up to go to the door, 'will certainly be Mons Graupius.'

IX. *The 'Tour'*

'Now THAT I HAVE HECTOR and Behag at home will we go
for our little tour?' asked Morag, to whom any sort of out-
ing, even a day's shopping, was a 'tour'.

'That's a good idea,' I agreed, 'but while we're about it
let's be ambitious. Let's go as far as Inverness and see some
shops.'

Morag and I had often talked of going away together
for a few days' holiday but always before she had pleaded
that her animals and poultry prevented her from leaving
the croft for more than a day. I was prepared for excuses now.

'Aye,' she agreed surprisingly; 'and we might even get
farther. I'd like to go to Edinburgh and see them little
penny-goin'-ins I seen when I was there a few years back.'

'You mean those slot machines you put a coin in and
get chocolate or something in return?' I asked.

'No, no, mo ghaoil. I mean them black and white birds they feed fish to at the zoo.'

Our tour was soon arranged. To save us the usual early morning bus ride and to make our journey scenically more interesting, Hector volunteered to take us to the mainland in his boat. He reckoned he could count on getting together a party of tourists who could be persuaded into thinking that the trip was exactly what they wanted and thus make it a financial success.

The day arranged for our tour broke unpromisingly grey and damp with flayed clouds working their way sluggishly over the hill tops and a rumpled line of sea stretching across the mouth of the bay. Only one or two tourists were waiting at the shore when Morag and I arrived there.

'What sort of a trip are we going to have?' I asked Erchy, who was acting as temporary crew for Hector.

'It'll be choppy enough out there when we get,' he replied, 'but we'll no be sayin' anythin' about that until we get the tourists aboard. It's calm enough here on the shore.'

Familiarity with the sea since I had come to the Hebrides had completely overcome my former terror: the prospect of a choppy passage I now found exhilarating. Erchy rowed us out in the dinghy to the *Wayfarer* where Hector had mugs of tea waiting for us in the the the fo'c'sle.

'Best fill up tse kettle again and we'll give tse rest tea when tsey come aboard,' said Hector. Erchy filled up the kettle from a rusty watercan and put it back on the Primus stove.

'How many people are you expecting to come today?' I asked.

'About twenty altogeszer, I believe,' Hector replied.

'As many as that? I thought you weren't allowed to carry more than twelve fare-paying passengers without a Board of Trade licence?'

'I'm not allowed to drown more tsan twelve fare-paying passengers,' Hector corrected me gravely. I chuckled, but his expression remained perfectly serious. It appears to be a curious legal anomaly that in this country any greenhorn can take up to twelve fare-paying passengers in any boat, be it held together by nothing more than paint and prayer, and so long as he does not drown more than the twelve he is not committing an offence in law; it is a very serious matter if he drowns thirteen. That, at any rate, is how the Hebridean boatmen interpret the law.

Hector finished his tea and popped his head up out of the fo'c'sle. 'Tsere's quite a few folks waiting on tse shore now,' he announced. He collected the cups and washed them in the kettle. 'Tsat'll put a bit of strength in tseirs for tsem,' he remarked happily.

Erchy hauled the dinghy alongside and jumped down into it. 'There's more than twenty there now,' he remarked as he pulled at the oars. 'I wonder will they all want to come?'

'If tsere's more tsan we can take tsen see and pick tse young ones, tsey's easier to get aboard if she turns bad on us,' called Hector.

The dinghy's stem crashed into the bow of *Wayfarer*.

'She's tsere when she bumps,' commented Hector sarcastically.

'Erchy's sometimes no very good at manuring the boat

alongside,' Morag murmured to me.

Half a dozen people came aboard, four sparsely haired though youngish men and two girls. One of the girls was a curvaceous blonde whom Hector's eyes appropriated as soon as he saw her.

'Here, Hector,' called Erchy, 'd'you know who's on the shore wantin' with us?'

'No, who?' demanded Hector.

'The pilgrims—Miss Flutter and Stutter. Will I get them?'

'God!' said Hector expressively. 'Are tsey goin' away?'

'They're goin' some place,' said Erchy, and added warningly: 'Pilgrims is as bad as ministers for making the weather blow up.'

'Aye,' Hector agreed, massaging his unshaven jaw perplexedly. He brightened. 'See if you can get tsem by tsemselves and tell tsem it's goin' to be awful wild,' he said.

'I've done that already,' said Erchy. 'They just told me it's a good forecast.'

Hector groaned. 'Maybe it was a good forecast for tse Bay of Biscay tsey heard,' he said. 'Ach, well, if you canna' leave tsem behind you'll just have to bring tsem, tsat's all.'

Miss Flutter and Miss Stutter came out with the next boatload. Miss Flutter greeted us effusively. She simply must, she insisted, sit outside in the breeze to stop her from feeling sick; she had brought her knitting for the same purpose.

'I find I simply must keep my mind occupied,' she said, pulling a half-knitted sleeve out of her bag and commencing work on it immediately. Miss Stutter managed a taut smile and twined her gloved fingers together ceaselessly.

By the time we had taken aboard the third boatload the sea outside had infected the bay with its restlessness and *Wayfarer* was beginning to rock tentatively at her moorings.

'I'm sure to be sick,' asserted a great cart-horse of a girl who sported a frugal pony-tail, and in preparation she draped herself into a suitable position. More boatloads of tourists were harvested from the shore, always with young women predominant, and not until we had more than thirty people squatting along either deck and littering the fore-peak did Hector call a halt.

'There's seven more still wantin',' said Erchy. 'They think I'm goin' back for them.'

Hector looked speculatively at his packed boat and then yearningly at the seven extra fares. 'Best go for tsem,' he said.

'No damty fear I'm not,' said Erchy relentlessly. 'They're all old or fat or lame so we'll be the better without them.' He clambered aboard and went forward to cast off the mooring as the engine throbbed into activity. *Wayfarer*'s bow commenced to dip a series of smug fare-wells to the disappointed tourists on the shore and then headed out of the bay.

'You can give her the gutty now,' Erchy shouted as he finished coiling ropes and picked his way carefully among the bodies back to the wheelhouse.

'You'd best make tse tea,' Hector said, 'before we get out of tse bay.'

'Here, here,' remonstrated Erchy, 'how am I goin' to serve tea round this lot. It'll all be spilled and wasted.'

'We've said tea was included in tse fare so we must offer it to tsem,' insisted Hector. 'Be quick now and let tsem have it before we get outside. It's no our fault tsen if tsey canna' drink it.'

Erchy grumbled a little more and then dived down below. I wedged myself in a corner of the wheelhouse and watched with mounting satisfaction the seas growing shaggier and shaggier as we approached the open water. Morag had found an old newspaper and was engrossed in reading the obituary notices. Hector leaned against the wheel, apparently steering with his backside, and riveted his eyes on the luxuriant tresses of the blonde. Erchy soon reappeared from the fo'c'sle with slopping mugs of milky tea which he thrust sulkily at the startled passengers. His arm also described a semi-circle with a tin of biscuits but the gesture was so repressive that no one had the courage to do anything but refuse. Some of the biscuits looked to me as though they had been refused for a long time.

Before we reached the black rocks, crenellated with shags, which flanked the entrance to the bay, *Wayfarer* had begun that confident surging and swinging motion with which a sturdy boat meets the challenge of the waves. It was not a savage sea but a snarling and defiant one and our course lay directly into the wind. The bow was soon lifting to each breaker, sagging down into the troughs and flinging lacy scarves of spray up over the half-decks. The passengers, amply clad in anoraks and waterproof trousers, appeared so far to be enjoying the cavorting of the boat. Right up on the foredeck a muscly young giant sat with his arms tightly encircling his emaciated girlfriend. Each time the bow dipped his arm tightened; it was debateable sometimes whether the noise we heard was the crackling of water under the stem head or the scrunching of the poor lassie's bones. The girl cart-horse leaned resolutely over the gunwale and waited for something to come up. Miss Flutter knitted industriously.

Suddenly a peculiar bumping sound became apparent. The two boatmen looked at each other questioningly.

'Tsat's tsat light anchor come loose,' said Hector. 'Best go and fix it.' Erchy started forward along the side deck, which was now wet and slippery.

Once aboard the *Wayfarer* the sexes seemed to have mutually agreed to separate and the starboard deck was lined with huddled girls while the smaller number of men spread themselves out in comparative comfort along the port deck. Erchy picked his way gingerly through the mass of girls, secured the anchor and came back the same way. We had not progressed very much farther when the bumping began again.

'You couldn't have done it properly, Erchy, it's loose again,' said Hector.

Erchy muttered imprecations under his breath and prepared to go forward.

'Erchy,' I suggested, 'wouldn't it be better, with the boat tossing about like this, if you went along the port deck. It's not so crowded.'

'No damty fear!' he replied. 'Those decks are slippery for me in gumboots.'

'That's why I suggested you should go along where the men are,' I said; 'after all, if you did happen to slip. . . .'

Erchy stared at me in serious surprise.

'What's the use to me of a lot of bald heads or crew-cuts if I lose my footing?' he demanded scathingly. 'I'm goin' where the women are so I'll have some hair to grab hold of.'

I dwindled back into my corner of the wheelhouse.

After about half an hour the Islands retired behind blinds of rain and the sea became perceptibly friskier. *Wayfarer's* motion began to have its inevitable effect. The cart-horse squandered herself upon the deck and when several of the others had laid listless heads on the shoulders of their companions Erchy, with great jubilation, was able to point out to Hector that the making of tea had indeed been a waste. I felt dreadfully sorry for poor Miss Stutter, who sat rigid beside her companion, staring with glazed eyes at the sea. Miss Flutter knitted on in desperation. The length of the sleeve had increased considerably during the half hour but whether it was due to her industry or whether it was sagging with the wet it was impossible to tell.

Hector was obviously anxious to get into conversation with his blonde so he left the wheel to Erchy and in a few moments was luring the blonde into the fo'c'sle. Erchy raised his eyebrows at me meaningly. Morag, who had appropriated the only seat in the wheelhouse, affected not to notice her nephew's disappearance.

'Here, see that rock we're just passin',' Erchy said to me through the side of his mouth after a swift glance at Morag. 'Take a good look at it.'

I stared obediently at an apparently isolated black rock rearing up out of the water a few yards offshore.

'Yes, but what about it?' I asked.

'You'd wonder at it now, wouldn't you?' asked Erchy.

I looked again but saw nothing curious about the rock which was black and jutty and sea-washed like so many other rocks and which had a small flat area of green moss, no more than two or three feet across, capping it.

'There doesn't appear to be anything unusual about it,' I said.

'Well, I daren't go closer in to let you look, but surely you can see the letters that's on it?'

'Good Lord!' I ejaculated. Inconceivably, on the dark face of the rock the tell-tale letters 'H.M.S.' had been painstakingly chipped.

'That's what I was meanin',' said Erchy, his voice betraying awe and admiration. 'You'd wonder at it bein' possible.'

I began to find it difficult to stay still for though I was wedged into a corner of the wheelhouse there was nothing for me to hold on to. Morag's eyes were closed as she rocked to the movement of the boat. Erchy clung to the wheel and as *Wayfarer* began leaping I was thrown repeatedly against him.

'Here,' expostulated Erchy, when a particularly violent lurch of the boat flung me against him so hard that his hand was wrenched from the wheel and *Wayfarer* swung beam to sea. 'Get you up on that shelf and stay there out of my way.' He indicated a shelf across the corner of the wheelhouse about halfway up the sides. I had to be helped up into it, and when I was deposited my legs would not reach the floor and I found there was absolutely nothing I might cling to.

'I shall fall,' I objected, and screamed, flinging out my arms to save myself as the wheelhouse canted treacherously to port. Erchy rammed the palm of his large hand into my diaphragm and fended me off as indifferently as if I had been a sack of meal. He seemed to find this position very stabilizing for himself and thus ignominiously I completed the journey.

When we arrived at the mainland pier Erchy and Hector abandoned us to rush off and sell their lobsters and to meet a party of campers they were expecting to take back to Bruach.

'See and remind Miss Peckwitt's fire to keep in,' were Morag's parting words to her nephew. Behag had the key of my cottage and so that I should not return to a cold, damp house, she had promised to send Hector to light the fire for me each day.

The pier was full of activity. Lobsters and crabs were being landed and sorted; baskets of fish were being dumped on the scale; the bell that indicated to buyers that fish was ready for auction was being rung imperiously; gulls swooped low and squealed their frustration as lorries were loaded high with dripping fish boxes; boats were being refuelled; trollies were being pushed hither and thither by apathetic porters; fish-box squirters were dreamily playing their hoses on stacks of empty boxes, recollecting themselves only to apologize to passers-by who might be absent-mindedly squirted, or to swear at the unquenchable dogs who were determined to help. Sundry urchins darted among the fishermen rescuing moribund crabs to fling triumphantly at the jettisoned loaves of Glasgow bread, still in their waxed wrappings, which floated in the harbour. I could think of no more suitable fate for Glasgow bread.

A trio of labourers were having some difficulty pushing a large barrel along the pier which, at the point they had reached, was slimy with oil and fish offal. The first of the men crouched down and gave a hefty push but his feet slid from under him and he lay flat on his stomach. It was a very rotund stomach. He picked himself up and swore colourfully at the pier. The second man obligingly thrust his weight behind the barrel but his feet too slid treacherously. His stomach was less rotund and perhaps as a consequence his abuse was even more colourful than that of his predecessor. The third man tried his strength and again exactly the same thing occurred. The trio stood surveying the obstinate barrel and abusing the pier in increasingly picturesque language, much to the amusement of a fry of young fishermen who had gathered to watch the spectacle.

'Here, you'd best be careful with your language,' shouted one of them facetiously. 'Likely the pier will be gettin' up and swearin' back at you.'

With an hour to spare before our train was due to leave, Morag could think of nothing but getting herself a cup of tea and left to weave her way through the bustle of the pier to the nearest tea-room. I turned into the butcher's first with a message from Peggy. One of the disadvantages of living in isolation is that when one does manage to get away, much of one's time is spent in transacting business for oneself and others in an effort to make the isolation more endurable. The butcher's shop was low-ceilinged, cool and dim, its floor heavily carpeted with fresh sawdust. A fat, slovenly woman was leaning torpidly on the scrubbed wooden counter, a shopping bag hanging limply from her arm.

'What'll I give you today, Mary?' asked the butcher.

'Ach, somethin' for their dinner.'

'What? Chops, steaming, roasting?'

'Ach, I don't know at all.'

'What did you have for your dinner yesterday?'

'Ach, stew.'

'Well, I'll give you a bit of mince today then, will I?'

He weighed out the meat and put it into the woman's bag, and watched her slouch out of the shop.

'There's some of the men hereabouts would get no dinner at all if I didn't see to it,' he hissed at me.

The butcher was an exceedingly devout man, speaking invariably on indrawn breaths that kept his mouth constantly prim, and no one but myself appeared to think the large picture of the Crucifixion which hung above the gory joints so tastefully arranged on the slab behind him at all incongruous.

I translated Peggy's complaint of 'Neilly says he's not goin' to put his teeth in just to eat the stuff we've been gettin' lately' into suitable cuts and joints, and went on to the chandler's shop which by contrast was cosy as a cabin. It was full of the rugged smells of tar and oil and twine and paint. The chandler, one of the finest characters I have ever encountered, was wearing a grubby white coat which to us who knew him proclaimed the season of the year just as accurately as the weather or the calendar. At the beginning of the tourist season his coat was new-starched and spotless; the chandler himself was correspondingly constrained. As the season advanced the coat became progressively limper and grubbier and its wearer daily more relaxed. At the end of the season the coat was abandoned for the winter and the chandler reverted to his normal happy self. He greeted me now with a genial smile and made a careful note of my order and then he leaned on the counter talking of the things that mattered: of the goings on of Bruach and the neighbourhood with which he was well acquainted; of the merits of different lamp oils; of the construction of a creel; of the fastidiousness of crabs which need fresh bait to lure them into a creel and yet which will pull off their own claws and eat them; of the less fastidious lobsters which are more easily tempted by salted or slightly smelly bait but have less cannibalistic tendencies. There were frequent interruptions to our conversation while he attended to the children, little girls mostly, who came in with their pennies to buy fish hooks for their boy friends to fish with off the pier.

'I'll bet,' the chandler said with a smile, 'they're for that young Jimsey. Looks like a little angel with his golden curls and blue eyes and all the girls want him for their boy friend.

The wee tartar just exploits the lot of them. He's that clumsy with the hooks anyway he's always losing them and some of the lassies haven't a penny left of their pocket money to buy sweeties for themselves.'

We chuckled together over the ways of love and it followed naturally that he should go on to speak of Hector.

'My, but I got the surprise of my life when I saw him walk in here today,' he said.

'Didn't you know he had come back to live in Bruach then?' I asked.

'That I didn't. In fact, I doubted if I'd ever see him again.'

I waited with raised eyebrows.

'Well, it's like this,' he told me. 'Hector, as perhaps you've heard, was never very quick at payin' his bills but I just let him go on for a while without botherin' him. They never amounted to much at a time, but when it came up to eighteen pounds I sent him a bill at last. Next time he was wantin' somethin' he came in here and promised to pay but he said he hadn't the money on him then, though I know fine he must have had or he'd never have been able to get as drunk as he did. The next time was just the same, he promisin' to pay, and the next time again and so it went on for five or six years till he went away. I sent him the bill a few times more but when it got to twelve years and never a word I gave it up as a bad job. Well then, today he walks in here, only a few minutes since. "Sandy," he says, "I'm owing you eighteen pounds and I've come to pay it." You could have knocked me down I was so surprised, but he put three five-pound notes and three one-pound notes down on the counter and asked for a receipt. I gave him a receipt quick enough but I was so happy to have got the eighteen pounds after all these years that I wanted to do something to make him happy too, so I took up the three fivers and I gave him back the three one-pound notes. It was worth it to see his face light up.' The chandler grinned benevolently.

Our gossip had lasted rather longer than it should and I had to hurry if I was to deliver a note that Johnny had asked me to give to the joiner. The road from the harbour was steep and I wished I had the same incentive as the fishermen in whose wake I toiled: the public bar was at the top of the hill and the way they were drawn towards it was like the force of gravity in reverse. I found the joiner's shed but the door was tight shut and there was little to indicate that any sort of business was carried on there except for a notice-board which bore the esoteric announcement:

NEW BOTTOMS	1/6d each
ditto, TARRED	2/3d each

I knocked at the door of a neighbouring cottage, from the garden of which two ragged-looking geese eyed me apprehensively, and enquired after the joiner. He had gone, I was told, with his family on a Sunday School picnic.

I rushed back down the hill to find Morag.

'Did you give the joiner Johnny's message?' she asked,

as we hurried to the station.

'No,' I told her. 'He's gone off on a Sunday School picnic.'

'What like of man is that then, goin' off on a Sunday School picnic on a Saturday,' she scoffed.

The guano-spattered train with its assemblage of covetous gulls was already in the station and we dived hastily for the shelter of the corridor. We found an empty compartment and barely had we seated ourselves when the train gave a jolt and started to move resolutely away from the platform. I held my watch to my ear, thinking it must have stopped, but there was far too much noise to hear anyway. Then the train stopped, vacillated for a while between jostlings and bumps and groaned slowly back into the station.

'What is all this shunting for?' I enquired of a flaccid porter who appeared to be rooted to the platform outside our compartment. He blinked, looked pallidly about him and then with an obvious shock of recollection informed me solemnly:

' 'Tis all for the sake of the fish, madam. Just for the sake of the fish.'

'I expect they've had to put us on to an extra fish van,' Morag interpolated. 'I was talkin' to a woman in the tea-room and she told me there'd been heavy landings today.' She produced a bag of peppermints and sat back, sucking contentedly.

'You mind,' she said reminiscently when the driver had let the engine have its head, 'that woman I was talkin' to in the tea-room? Well, her man's a fisherman and he was in today with a good catch, but do you know what that man is gettin' for his tea tonight?'

'Boiled fish,' I guessed.

'No, but fish fingers—them artificial fish out of deep freezers. And he loves them, she says, and so does the rest of the fishermen.'

'Good gracious!'

'Aye,' agreed Morag indignantly. 'Them things! For a man! And not a bit of taste to them at all, until they come back.'

I have an unfortunate habit of falling asleep on trains and so I was soon startled by Morag's shaking me and telling me to get ready to alight. We were breaking our journey so that I could visit a dentist and so that Morag could seek out a builder's yard where there might be second-hand sinks and basins for sale, for now that Hector was home she clung to the hope that he would put in piped water for her.

The delightful lady with whom we had arranged to spend the night heaped our beds with eiderdowns as though the temperature were several degrees below zero, although it was but mid-September, and heaped our plates with food as though we had been starved. 'Oh my, I wish I had two stomachs,' sighed Morag greedily when she had eaten.

The dentist obligingly fitted me in without a previous appointment. He was a charming man and when his receptionist showed me into his homely surgery he was sitting on the floor playing happily with an adorable little puppy. He was wearing a starched white jacket, bedroom slippers and no socks. I sat in the chair and waited timidly while he gathered up the puppy and carried it over to its basket. He put it in, patted it and told it to stay there and then came and stood over me. Taking an instrument from an array on a nearby shelf he told me to open wide and began to probe. 'Ah, yes . . . perfect, perfect . . . now puppy . . . naughty puppy! Stay there puppy . . . nice puppy. . . .' Even rolling my eyes to their extremities I could not see what the puppy was up to but my attention was caught by a shelf above that on which the instruments were arrayed. It looked to be a species of museum shelf and reposing on it was a collection of awe-inspiring relics of previous clients. The dentist continued with his inspection. 'Good teeth you have . . . yes. . . .' He jerked away suddenly. 'Puppy! Naughty puppy!' He turned and shook the instrument at it admonishingly. 'When he wants me to play with him he has a habit of nipping my ankles and his teeth are terribly sharp,' he vouchsafed by way of explanation. He bent over me again but, changing his mind, he picked up the puppy and stowed it again in its basket.

'Now stay there, puppy,' he bade it firmly. 'My wife usually looks after it but she's gone off to hospital to visit her mother,' he said companionably. 'And my secretary's away home now.' The puppy sat in his basket looking appealingly vague. The dentist resumed his inspection. 'Aye, yes, now there's a wee holey there . . . no more I think. Ouch!' he jerked away again.

'Puppy!' He sounded really cross and looked about him helplessly for a moment as though wondering whether to put down the instruments and chastise the offender. His eye suddenly lighted on the museum shelf. Surreptitiously he flicked off one of the relics, which rattled across the surgery with the puppy gambolling happily after it. The dentist breathed a sigh of relief and concentrated his attention on stopping my tooth. As a retriever the puppy was not a conspicuous success and there were only one or two relics remaining on the shelf when I took my leave.

In Edinburgh we spent our days and nights being entertained by past residents of Bruach, by relatives of present residents of Bruach and by Morag's own innumerable friends and relations, so much so that I saw hardly anything of the city and Morag did not find time to renew her acquaintance with the penguins. On our return journey we touched Inverness briefly on a hot, busy day with the buses grinding heavily along and ice cream trodden over the pavements. Inverness suffers too much from the cult of the laird to be popular with Islanders and when they go away they prefer the indiscriminate affability of Edinburgh and Glasgow. At Morag's suggestion we carried on to Dingwall, which is a delightfully scatterbrained little town wavering between East-coast industry and West-coast indolence. Coming out of the station we were confronted with what looked like the preparations for a Guy Fawkes bonfire but which we found was the Seaforth memorial to the battle of Cambrai. But Dingwall is really dominated by the church tower with its four clocks of which, during the time we were there, no two were in agreement and not one was correct. Our landlady was no generous Highlander; she did not smother us with eiderdowns nor overtax our stomachs, but she was the only landlady I have ever come across who had the courage to put a supply of the day's newspapers in the lavatory in addition to an ample supply of toilet paper. I like Dingwall for its individuality and for its decorous bustle but mostly it will linger in my memory as the place where at night the men stand so still on the street corners that even the dogs get confused.

The train journey from Dingwall to the West is beautiful indeed and the halts frequent enough to allow it to be fully assimilated. I slept most of the way and roused myself for lunch to find that our compartment was now shared by a corpulent old Highlander and a heavily built, masculine-looking woman. The man was dressed in black suit, black hat, black shiny boots and with a snowy Woolworth's handkerchief in his breast pocket. I know it was a Woolworth's handkerchief because I had just bought a dozen for Erchy. When he was not conversing with Morag in the Gaelic he sat self-consciously in his corner staring at the pictures of Morecambe and Bognor Regis which decorated the compartment. He looked as though he had left his croft and his bible only for a few hours and was already wearying to return to them. I discovered he had been travelling the world for the past eighteen months visiting his scattered children and was only now on his way home. The woman was wearing an amorphous raincoat and a deer-stalker and she was so engrossed in a novelette with a lurid love scene backing that she appeared to be oblivious of our presence and even of the attractions of Morecambe and Bognor Regis.

We were back to contentious seagulls; back to 'Tea-rooms' (instead of restaurants) with their stale cakes that looked as though they had been kept on a shelf for six months and taken down and dusted only occasionally. The drizzly rain was full of salt; boats bumped against the slip; ropes were flung; the men's oilskins flapped and crackled. We squelched over seaweed to the ferry. I saw Morag aboard and then asked the ferryman if he could wait while I nipped into the shop on the pier. I had bought a large vacuum jar and I thought it would be a good idea to get it filled with ice cream for the children of Bruach who rarely got the chance to taste it. The youth in the shop considered the capacity of the jar and finally decided that two family bricks would compress suitably. The boy took the bricks and the jar to the back of the shop. He was gone for rather a long time and I could see the ferrymen were becoming restless.

'Please hurry,' I called; 'the ferry is waiting.'

He appeared hastily, rather red in the face, and handed me the jar.

'I had no idea it was going to take so long,' I said testily as I handed him the money.

'Ach, but d'you see, I had to melt them first to get them to go in,' he consoled me fatuously.

I hurried down to the ferry.

'Miss Peckwitt! Miss Peckwitt! Mattam!' I stopped. A cadaverous oilskinned figure was lumbering towards me.

'Miss Peckwitt, am I spekink to?' He was very, very Highland.

'Yes,' I admitted. 'Do you want something?'

'Would you be goin' back to Bruach now, mattam?'

I admitted I would.

'In that case would you be takink a wee message to Willy John MacRae? The phone iss not workink.'

I said I would.

'You will tell him then that there iss a corp to come over for him tomorrow on the boat.'

'A what did you say?'

'A corp, mattam, to come over. . . .'

The ferrymen were revving the engine impatiently.

'Yes,' I cut in, 'I know, but what is it you said was to come over in the boat?'

'A corp, mattam.'

'A corp?'

'Indeed yes.' He could not conceal that he thought me very unintelligent. 'Willy John's uncle has died in Glasgow and his corp is to come over tomorrow,' he explained patiently.

'Oh!' I exclaimed. 'You mean a corpse!'

He looked at me pityingly.

'Mattam,' he rebuked me gently. 'I was spekink in the sinkular.'

X. *The 'Herring Fish'*

'THE TROUBLE WITH THIS PLACE,' complained the local vet exasperatedly, 'is that every single soul in it is a fierce individualist. Other townships manage to work together for their own good, but Bruach, never!'

The veterinary surgeons of the Hebrides are splendid men doing gruelling work over a vast area for long hours, often with little consideration or co-operation, yet they are unfailingly helpful, good-humoured and appear to be completely tireless. Our Island vet was no exception, but his exasperation was occasioned by the fact that he had spent a long day under appalling weather conditions chasing over mile upon mile of moor and bog trying to get within 'stabbing' distance of cattle that were as wild as the hills that bred them. He had out-manœuvred aggressive mothers with calves at foot; stalked refractory two-year-olds that had never before submitted to human touch; thrown himself upon young calves that fled on nimble legs from anything that had not horns and shaggy hair. In all this he had been hampered by a pack of vociferous Bruachites who, unable to agree as to the best way to catch a beast, had each gone about it in his own way; and by a pack of equally vociferous dogs which, frantic with excitement, had streaked in and out among the distraught beasts taking surreptitious nips at their heels.

'It's one thing to hold a beast when it's half-mad, but it's another when there's a dog chewing at his tail,' was another complaint the vet made; a complaint well justified by the number of rolls of coarse hair from the tips of tails that were later to be seen strewing the moors.

For such a round-up of cattle other villagers, as the vet pointed out, had combined to fence off cattle 'parks'. Bruach had never aspired to anywhere other than the school playground but, to everyone's indignation, the present teacher had protested against its use for penning cattle, maintaining that the uproar distracted the pupils and that the language they could not help overhearing, particularly when one of the more recalcitrant beasts managed repeatedly to evade its captors, was altogether unsuitable.

Another way in which Bruach lagged behind other townships was in its reluctance to run a joint sheep stock. This arrangement whereby each crofter has an equal share in a common stock on the hill, one member of the community being employed as shepherd, appeared to work harmoniously in other places. Bruach preferred to carry on as their fathers and grandfathers before them, each man having a few sheep on the hill and shepherding them whenever he felt the need or the urge to do so. It was a method which meant the flock was being constantly separated and harried from place to place, for however unco-operative their owners may have been the Bruach sheep still retained the instinct to flock together. Half-hearted proposals to merge stocks had been put forward from time to time but they were always resisted for a variety of reasons. They had felt their resistance to be amply justified when they heard of a stranger who, having taken over a croft in a neighbouring village and with it the share of the sheep stock, had ingenuously declared his annual profit from the stock on his income tax returns much to the interest of the Inland Revenue Authorities and much to the consternation of the rest of the holders.

If the Bruachites had shown more spirit of co-operation they might have achieved a Public Hall of some sort. They might even have managed a piped water supply instead of one house in three having an abundance of water while the rest depended on moody springs. Though the inability to work together appeared to be congenital with the majority of the villagers yet it rarely developed into anything more serious than peevish wrangling. The two main causes of perceptible friction in Bruach were centred on the boats in the tourist season and in the herring fishing season, though if there was a glut of either tourists or of herring the crews managed to work together with the utmost cordiality, the idea being that it did not matter much which boat netted them so long as they were not allowed to get away. It was when there was a scarcity of either that any trouble flared up.

Between *Wayfarer*, Hector's boat, and *Seagull*, the boat of which Erchy and deaf Ruari, Morag's brother, each had a half share, there was at times bitter rivalry. They each took tourists for trips in the season. They each fished herring when it came into the loch. Their battles over tourists not only provided much entertainment for the rest of the village but more than once resulted in neither boat getting a trip because the passengers were afraid to risk going on the water with such fierce-sounding men. Deaf Ruari was mainly responsible for their apprehension for though he was an extremely forbearing old man normally, the power of his lungs undoubtedly increased in proportion as his wrath and the sparse white hairs on his face could bristle most aggressively. At such times one could not wonder at the tourists preferring to admire the scenery from the safety of the shore.

As the tourist season came to an end so the boat crews gradually became more amicable, helping to haul up each other's dinghies, respecting each other's lobster ground and frequently reporting where good catches were to be obtained. Then the herring would come in and the antagonism would spring up again.

Herring appear to be creatures of habit and they usually shoaled into Bruach waters some time in April for a couple of weeks and then disappeared until the autumn. The Bruachites took little interest in April herring. They wanted their fish for salting and the autumn herring, being less oily, took the salt better. Round about September the previous year's supply would be finished, or, if it were not completely finished, the fish that were left would be thrown out on to the croft for the cows, so that one became accustomed to the sight of a cow standing chewing at a herring as a man chews at a cigar. The empty barrels would then be placed under a convenient waterfall to get thoroughly clean. (In an Island where the hills are full of streams there is never any difficulty in finding at least a cascade of water for each family's barrel.) The herring nets would then be taken down from the rafters where they had been stored since their 'mothproofing' at the end of their last season. The Bruachites mothproofed their nets by the simple method of leaving them in sacks or boxes for a time at the back of the house where the men could urinate on them. This very effective method of mothproofing is not, it seems, confined to herring nets; I know of one lady who gave away her hand-woven tweed suit after spending a winter holiday in a small weaving village and deducing the reason for the weaver's daily collection of pails of urine from their neighbours.

On calm, cool, moonlit nights with the sea lisping on the shingle shore, the noise of herring playing in the loch is a beautiful and exciting sound. A sound to be evoked on hot, parcel-burdened days in town or when enduring the stuffy torture of a long train journey. It is as though the shoal tickles the surface of the sea and makes it bubble with laughter. On just such a night of calm I was returning home from a ceilidh with Morag when Erchy's voice hailed me.

'We'll be thinkin' of ceilidhin' with you tomorrow night,' he said.

'Good,' I replied with polite warmth. 'Who's we?'

'Me, and Johnny and maybe one or two others,' he enlightened me generously. 'The loch's teemin' with herrin' and we'll need to get after them before it's away for the winter.'

'The herring's in already?' I exclaimed.

'Surely! Are you no hearin' it?' I had to admit that until he had mentioned it I had not heard any unusual sound. 'Aye, but the noise of herrin' is like that,' said Erchy. 'Unless your ears is tuned in to it you can miss it altogether.' I paused now, and listened rapturously.

The following morning when I rowed out to lift my lobster creel two groups of men were busy preparing their nets for shooting in the evening. Erchy, Angus and deaf Ruari comprised one group and Hector and Duncan, the son of the postmistress, the other. The distance between them emphasized that the period of camaraderie was already beginning to wane. I went over to talk to Hector.

'No lobster, I see,' he greeted me.'

'None today.'

'Nor yesterday, I'm tsinkin'.'

'No, not yesterday.'

'No indeed, when tse herrin's in tse loch it drives everytsin' away. I've seen whales in here, killers at tsat, and a big shoal of herrin' has come in and frightened tsem away out of it for tseir lives. It's as true as I'm here.'

I was pondering this unlikely information when Nelly,

the daughter of Elly, and consequently known as 'Nelly-Elly', came hurrying down to the shore. NellyElly ran the post office.

'They're wantin' you to go to the hills with the pollis,' she panted. 'There's been an accident.'

'I'll bet you tsat will mean a corpse,' said Hector glumly.

'It does so. A man's fallen and killed himself.' She paused for a few moments while we reacted to the news and then continued irately: 'I don't know whatever came over that Tom-Tom. Just because he finds a corpse he feels he should be able to tell me how to do my work. He kept ringing me up at the kiosk when I had a long distance call occupyin' the line and tellin' me I was to cut short the call because he had an urgent message for the pollis. Urgent, he said! I refused to do it. "It's no urgent at all," I told him, "the man's already dead." '

We approved her assessment of the situation by nodding our heads. 'The pollis will be down in half an hour,' she added soberly.

'Is Tom-Tom goin' back with them?' asked Duncan.

'No, he says he's not fit to go.'

'Do tsey know where tse body is, tsen?' demanded Hector, who was still very sulky with the police because he had recently been fined for carrying more than the stipulated twelve passengers in his boat. 'I'm no waitin' about for tsem while tsey go lookin' for it. I'll take tsem tsere and leave tsem, just. Tsey can walk home.'

'You'd best tell them that yourself,' said NellyElly with a toss of her head. 'Or if you don't want the job I can give it to Erchy.'

'To hell with tsat,' responded Hector. A great bone of contention between the two boats was that since the wily Hector had taken NellyElly's son, Duncan, to work with him he had naturally fallen in for all the telephoned boat bookings, there being only one telephone line to Bruach.

'I'd been tsinkin' I'd get home to my dinner and take a wee snooze tsis afternoon,' Hector mumbled lugubriously. 'We'll be up all night at tse herrin' and I didn't get to bed tsis mornin' till tse back of four.'

'Four o'clock isn't all that late for you,' I retorted. 'Behag tells me you're reading until about three every morning.'

'Aye, it was no awful late right enough, but I'm feelin' a wee bitty tired just tse same. I tsink I'll come up to tse cottage with you, seein' we can't get home, will I? And you'll make us a strupak?'

'What about you, Duncan?' I asked. 'Are you coming for a strupak too?' Duncan was large-boned, thin and dark, with a metallic-looking moustache. Whenever I spoke to him he looked at the ground. I got the impression that he thought his eyes so bold and bright that he conscientiously dipped them as one dips the headlights of a car.

The two men accompanied me to the cottage and while they drank tea and munched thick slabs of fruit cake I packed a few sandwiches for them. The way the Bruach men were inclined to go out in their boats for long spells without taking any food distressed me. I could only assume that their tummies had been too maltreated to be sensitive to mealtimes, for they just did not seem to notice hunger. Hector, who was wandering in and out of the kitchen with his half-full cup of tea, suddenly perceived the silver buttons of the policemen and went off, cup in hand, to meet them.

'Tsere tsey are, nice as you like to me today,' he muttered when he came in to deposit his cup and collect his sandwiches. 'Fine you one day and hire your boat tse next day to sweeten you. Tsat's tse pollis all over. But I'm damty sure tsey're no keepin' me away from tse herrin'. Corpse or no corpse, I'll be back for tsat.'

I watched the weather as anxiously as the men. I loathe salt herring, but the crofters consider it not only a necessity but a delicacy. If it blew up there would be no herring fishing and the excitement that had threaded its way through the village with the coming of the shoal would die away. All morning the sun and the rain argued with each other while the wind played a bustling arbiter, but with the afternoon the sun finally triumphed and calmness again spread itself over the loch. As I fed the hens in the evening, *Wayfarer*, seeming downcast by her mission, struggled up the shadowed loch leaving an arrowed wake and, soon after she had moored up, a lorry which had been waiting at the shore juddered past the cottage with its gruesome burden, covered in tarpaulins. Another lorry full of glowing, gaily waving men, presumably members of the rescue party, followed shortly afterwards, and then the car with the policemen. Hector and Duncan called in at the cottage on their way home. Duncan looked a little white and strained, Hector merely looked smug.

'You see all tsat load of men goin' up tse road in tse lorry?' he demanded of me. I nodded. 'Well, every one of tsose men I brought home in my boat in one load, and tsere was over twenty of tsem without tse pollis.'

'How did you get away with that?' I asked him.

'Well, tsey came down to tse shore and tsey had tse body so tsey put tsat on board. Tsat was all right. Tsen came tse sergeant. "All aboard, we've finished for tse night, lads," he told tsem, nice as you like. When eleven was on tse boat I held up my hand. Says I, "I'll have to come back for tse rest of you, I'm no allowed to carry more tsan twelve on tsis boat, I have no licence." "Where's your twelve?" asks tse sergeant, and he looks cross. "Eleven of you and him in tse tarpaulin," says I. "Tsat makes my twelve." Tse sergeant looks at me and he says, "Tsat's a fine big boat you have tsere, Hector, and tsough tse law says twelve it's a daft law." "It was no so daft a few weeks back," I told him. "Why, tsat boat's safe enough with fifty aboard," he says. "On you get with you, boys." "It's your responsibility," I says. "My responsibility entirely," he agrees, so off we go, happy as you like. Ach, but tsey'd been trampin' the hills and climbin' around all day lookin' for tse body and they didn't want to be left tsere in tse dark. Tsey knew I'd take my time before I'd go back for tsem.'

'The sergeant was quite friendly, then,' I said with a smile.

'Friendly!' echoed Hector. 'He was tsat friendly when I offered him a sandwich he near bit tse hand off me. Aye, but I know what I'll do if tsey catch me with more tsan twelve again. I'll say all tse rest over twelve is corpses.'

I mentioned to Hector before he left that Erchy and his friends were expecting to ceilidh at the cottage that evening.

'We'll maybe be tsere ourselves too,' he promised. I was perfectly well aware that it was not my company that was being sought but only the convenient shelter of my cottage. The Bruach herring fishing was done from dinghies and the net was set and reset every hour or so, the crew coming ashore between settings. My cottage, so close to the shore and to their nets, was ideally situated for them, and I resolved that as soon as Morag and Behag, who were also coming to ceilidh with me that evening, had left for their own home I would retire to bed and leave the herring fishermen in possession to brew themselves tea and make themselves comfortable as they wished.

While Morag and Behag were still with me the first lot of fishermen trooped in and flopped down on the available chairs and on the floor. There were Erchy and Johnny and Angus, nearly always an inseperable trio in any evening ploy; there were Tom-Tom and a cousin from Glasgow. Their eyes were shining and they all looked drunk, but they were drunk only with the excitement of the occasion.

'The loch's stiff with fish of some sort,' pronounced Erchy.

'If Hector catches herrin' tonight I'll no get him to bed for a week,' mourned Behag.

'No man needs to sleep when he's catchin' herrin','

Erchy told her. 'I've stuck at the herrin' for a week near enough without gettin' a wink of sleep and never felt tired. So long as you're catchin' them it's all right. It's when you're not you get tired.'

I noticed the absence of deaf Ruari whom I had expected to be there as skipper of the *Seagull*. 'Doesn't Ruari go herring fishing at all?' I asked.

'Ach, he cannot come because Bella's afraid to sleep by herself. Honest, the way that man looks after his wife you'd think there was a subsidy on her.'

'How come you to be here then, Angus?' asked Morag. 'Isn't Ishbel on her own and in no fit state to be left?'

'I got my brother to stay beside her tonight,' Angus excused himself.

There were noises outside and soon Hector, Duncan and Sandy Beag were adding their voices to the general teasing and argument which inevitably accompanies an impromptu ceilidh like this.

'You'd best see to your nets,' said Morag as she tied a scarf over her head in readiness to go home. 'You've been in here over an hour, Erchy. You'll no catch herrin' in Miss Peckwitt's kitchen.'

'The way you women talk about the fish it's a wonder we ever catch a single one,' cut in Sandy Beag irascibly.

'Oh, stop frettin' yourself Sandy,' Morag told him. 'Erchy himself has been speakin' of the herrin' by name, have you not, Erchy?'

'I believe I did,' admitted Erchy.

'Then he'll no catch any the night,' predicted Sandy earnestly.

'There are quite a lot of superstitions connected with herring fishing, aren't there?' I began, and stopped as I met a glare from Sandy.

'Aye, there's a few right enough,' Erchy said. 'One is that you mustn't go fishin' for them on Fridays. Another that you musn't let a woman cross your path when you're on your way.'

'I thought it was only a red-haired woman?' I interpolated.

'A red-haired woman's all right for ordinary fish, but herrin' are more particular. Any woman will put off herrin' so they say. Then, you mustn't point at them when you hear them playin'. You've got to show where they are without pointin'. And you must never turn the boat against the clock when you're goin' out to the net. That's the only one I take any notice of myself.'

'You mark what I say, Erchy, you'll no get the fish you're wantin' tonight the way you're after speakin' of them,' Sandy reiterated.

After Morag and Behag had gone, I went to bed and heard vaguely throughout the night the heavy clumping of sea-boots in the kitchen and at times the disturbing sound of raised voices. When I got up there was a lovely fire burning in the grate, the kettle was hissing on the hob and the cups they had used had been washed and put away. News came later that the night's fishing had yielded one herring.

The following night I was in bed when they arrived, but I had told them to make use of the kitchen. I slept soundly and the dawn was only a paler shadow over the sea when there came a thumping on the door of my room.

'What is it?' I called sleepily.

'Were you not sayin' you were wantin' to get a lift to the mainland if you could, so as to get your car?' Erchy's voice shouted.

I grunted that I had indeed said so. The repairs to 'Joanna' were now completed, the garage had said, and she was ready for collection.

'Well, now's your chance. We've 'phoned for a lorry to take our fish and it'll be here in half an hour. I'm away now.'

I got up quickly and went into the kitchen. The table was strewn with dirty cups—no saucers—and the floor was littered with cigarette stubs. There were only elusive red cinders under a mound of warm peat ash in the grate. An abandoned cap hung on a chair, glistening with herring scales in the lamplight. I pushed the dishes into the sink and brewed coffee. The air of the kitchen was still thick with tobacco fumes and my mouth felt as though I too had been smoking all night. I finished my coffee as I heard the noise of an engine, and threw on my coat. The hens and Bonny would have to wait until I got back.

Hector loomed up in the open doorway. He looked in surprise at my attire. 'Are you comin' with us?' he asked, his eyes signifying immense pleasure at the prospect.

'I thought it was Erchy who told me to hurry,' I said. 'Are you sharing a lorry between you?'

'No, indeed,' he replied. 'We're havin' a lorry each.'

'You must have got a lot of herring,' I complimented him.

'Well, we got a few cran.'

'And how many did Erchy get?'

'Ach, he got very few herrin'. Mostly mackerel it was in tseir net, tsough I don't know why. Tsey didn't set tseir nets much different to our own.'

'Sandy will be more superstitious than ever,' I said. 'But Erchy will be disappointed.'

'Aye, he was disappointed right enough,' he said with spurious sympathy, and then added brightly, 'God! I could hear him swearin' away tsere all night. I believe he made a swear for every mackerel he took out of tse net.' He chuckled. 'You may as well come on our lorry,' he went on. 'It'll be tsere before Erchy's.'

Erchy bounded in at this juncture, looking a little cross. 'Are you ready?'

'Yes, I'm ready, but Hector says his lorry will be there before yours, and I must try to get back here as soon as possible.'

'Damty sure it won't be there before my lorry,' Erchy said combatively.

'Damty sure it will,' responded Hector.

'I'm going on the one that's in front at this moment,' I said firmly, and went out and got into the cab, leaving the two still arguing in the kitchen.

The foremost lorry was loaded with herring and ready to start. The mackerel lorry was only now coming up from the shore. Duncan and Sandy, the latter looking very self-satisfied, hoisted themselves to the back of the lorry with the fish. Hector jumped in beside me. 'Come on! Give her tse gutty,' he urged the driver. 'Tsere's a good dram in it for you if we beat tsem to it.'

'Why are you so bothered about beating Erchy's lorry?' I asked as the driver roared the engine full ahead. 'Surely if he has mackerel his catch won't affect the price you'll get for your herring, or the other way round.'

'Indeed it will so!' Both the driver and Hector turned on me indignantly. 'If he gets tsere first with his mackerel tsey won't be nearly so keen to pay high prices for our herrin'. Oh, tsey'll buy tsem, right enough, but tsey're no big buyers and tsey cannot take a lot of fish. We could very easily lose by it. Y'see, Erchy has some herrin' himself. He'll sort tsem on tse way in and if tse buyers tsinks tsere's only a few tsey'll pay him top price. Tsen when tsey see us come in with our lot tsey'll tsink tsere must be plenty more so tse price will drop.' He turned to the driver. 'Make every bit of speed you can, Neilly,' he exhorted him. The driver nodded understandingly.

Whilst we were on the narrow road we had no difficulty in keeping our lead. The horn of the following lorry was sounded repeatedly but whenever we came to a passing place our driver took the middle of the road and frustrated any attempt on the part of the other driver to get ahead. I wondered if Erchy was in the cab of the lorry similarly exhorting its driver and promising a similar reward. As we careered along at furious speed my hair began to stand on end. I knew the tortuous Bruach road and treated it with respect. The lorry driver must have been equally familiar with it but this morning he treated it with contempt. The lorry was senile and unbuoyant and through the gaps between the floorboards I glimpsed the rough road planed by our speed. When we reached the narrow strip of road with the sea a sheer drop of eighty feet below I cowered into my seat and had I not been firmly wedged between Hector and the driver I believe I would have essayed a jump from the offside door. When we came out on the high road I felt a certain amount of relief though our speed was still perilous.

Hector glanced behind him. 'He's comin' alongside,' he told the driver. 'Head him off!' But the driver, to whom I hoped sanity had perhaps returned with the constraint of a main road, refused to swerve more than a foot or two. The cab of the second lorry drew inexorably up on us, its grim-faced driver visible crouched over his wheel. Our own driver increased his speed so that the two lorries kept their bonnets dead level. I was surprised to see that Erchy was not in the cab of the other lorry, but by turning to look out of the rear window I could see him and his cronies standing up among the piled mackerel, looking desperately streamlined with their caps back to front and their clothes flat against their bodies. They were all fiercely gesticulating and mouthing what I knew would probably be wild insults at the men on the back of our own lorry. I saw Erchy pick up a mackerel and hurl it vengefully towards us. I saw his cronies instantly pick up fish and hurl them likewise, and almost immediately I saw the herring raining down on them from our own lorry. I glanced at Hector but he was intent on chewing his fingers, his eyes glued to the road. It was fortunate that it was so early in the morning and there was no traffic; if there had been I doubted if our drivers, in the mood they were in, would have got out of the way. I looked round again as we passed a tinker encampment beside the road. Two of the tinkers stood outside and I saw their expressions change rapidly from outrage to delight as they too were pelted with fish.

'Two loads of mixed herring and mackerel,' announced the fish buyers' assistant when the lorries finally halted at the pier.

'Here, no!' protested Hector, hurrying to the back of the lorry. His mouth dropped open as he saw his confederates standing shame-faced among the herring and mackerel. He went closer. 'How in hell did tsis happen?' he asked, dazedly.

'Ach, we just had a bit of an argument,' Erchy told him. 'It's settled now.'

'God!' ejaculated Hector when he had heard the full story. 'Tsat's a joke right enough. I wish I'd seen tse faces of tsose tinks when tse fish hit tsem.'

'Indeed, we near fell off the lorry ourselves laughin' at them,' chuckled Johnny.

The fish dealer paid them their money and they all went off happily together to wait in some congenial place for the pubs to open so that they could spend it. Only the two drivers were left and they stayed in their lorries glaring at each other lugubriously until they were gestured away by impatient fish porters.

'Ach, them Bruach men,' said the fish buyer in my ear, 'there's no sense in them at all. I believe they're as mad as I don't know what.'

I went to collect 'Joanna' and allowed my body to untense itself slowly as I drove homeward. The morning mist was rising from the hill corries and from the tumbling, bracken-fringed burns. Above the mountains to the east the sunlit clouds had the metallic look of crumpled tinfoil. At the tinker encampment the family were gathered round a fire and a big fat woman was flourishing a frypan. A most delectable smell of fried herring was wafted across the road.

XI. *Bread and Uisge-Beatha*

'THE HEBRIDEANS,' declaimed the holidaymaker from Glasgow, 'are very pure, you know.'

I didn't know, so I waited for her to explain. She had been coming to Bruach for a holiday every winter for the last ten years, long before I had known of its existence, so she really should have known what she was talking about. I wondered if she would next trot out the myth that crofters are hard working. She did. 'Bruach in my opinion,' she summed up, 'is an ideally happy, healthy, moral and law-abiding community.' Janet, her landlady, slid me a wary glance from the corners of her eyes.

'Indeed, and isn't it nice to hear someone say that?' she asked me.

'Oh, but I mean every word of it,' enthused the visitor. 'I should simply love to live in Bruach.'

It is curious that the people who express a longing to live in the Hebrides usually avoid doing so. So far as I knew, the only people who had made any real effort to find a home in Bruach had been middle-aged spinsters like myself, and for this the fact that the village had more than its share of middle-aged bachelors may have been largely responsible.

It was a chilly evening in November; an evening of chastened calm after a day and night of such storm and fury that when I had looked out of my cottage that morning I had been faintly surprised to see the outer islands still occupying their normal positions. Janet, the visitor and myself were comfortably ensconced in the visitor's sitting-room awaiting the arrival of the grocery van which visited the village each week. Though there was a small general shop in Bruach, the owner of which claimed to sell everything from 'fish to chemistry', many of the crofters preferred to go to the van for the bulk of their purchases. The main reason for this, I believe, was that it came on specified days at more or less specified times so that everyone could congregate round it when it stopped and indulge in a 'good crack', as they called a gossip. To wander up to the shop when the chances were that you would meet no one but the grocer or his family was not considered nearly such good entertainment. Wild weather on van days gave the excuse to drop in at the houses of friends who lived near the road and to chat over a cup of tea while listening for the long-drawn-out blast of the horn by which the driver always announced his arrival.

'My, but the van's very late,' observed Janet, getting up

to put more peats on the fire.

The outer door opened and a man's voice shouted.

'Is that you, Murdoch? Come away in,' called Janet.

Old Murdoch opened the door and put his head inside. He obviously had not shaved for days and his face looked as though it had been planted by the Forestry Commission. His nose reared through the growth like the beginning of a forest fire.

'What's that you're sayin'?' enquired Janet.

'I'm sayin' it's no good you waitin' here,' he told us. 'The van's away back home. You'll no be seein' him tonight.'

'Why ever's that?' asked Janet.

'Indeed, he gave no explanation at all,' said the old man. 'He stopped once just at the top of the village and then he turned the van and went off home without a word to anybody.'

'Well, well,' murmured Janet. 'I wonder whatever has happened.'

'They're sayin' there's a dance on at Sheehan and he's wantin' to get back in time for it,' said Murdoch.

There was a gasp of disapproval from the visitor.

'That's no good enough,' observed Janet indignantly. 'Leaving us all without supplies just to go to a dance.'

'Aye, there's some of them awful wild about it,' agreed Murdoch. 'NellyElly's sayin' she hasn't a bitty sugar in the house to take with their tea. And Anna-Vic's sayin' she hasn't a biscuit left though she's bought nine pounds this week already.'

'Nine pounds of biscuits! In a week!' repeated the visitor incredulously.

'Aye, but she has a big family,' Janet said defensively.

'Her own mother had a big family too,' exclaimed Murdoch. 'And I never saw her buy a biscuit in her life. She baked everythin' herself on the girdle.' Murdoch took his pipe from his pocket, brandished it compellingly and settled himself on a chair. 'Never a shop biscuit nor a shop loaf went into that house and look at the fine family she reared.'

'No, but the vans didn't come in those days,' argued Janet.

'No, and there wasn't so many pensions to pay for all the stuff, either,' retorted Murdoch.

Janet smiled disapprovingly. 'Murdoch would like to see us all back to the old days when women did nothin' but work all day long,' she said. 'That's why no woman would marry him.'

I said good night, leaving Murdoch reminiscing happily with the visitor. Janet came with me to the door.

'I wonder when the van will come now?' I asked, though aware of the triviality of the question.

'Dear knows,' answered Janet, 'but there'll be some miscallin' of that man if it was nothin' but a dance took him from the village.'

I thanked her automatically for the strupak. 'Don't thank me for that, my dear, it was just thrown at you,' she disclaimed modestly. 'You'll be at Jeannac's weddin' party tomorrow?' she reminded me. I assured her that I would be.

There was now a nip of frost in the air, and across the

vastness of the sky shooting stars dodged brilliantly as though hectored by the presumptuous moon. Beyond the bay the scattered lighthouses flashed like jewels against the rustling dark velvet of the water while close at hand the noise of the burn swelled and diminished as it was caught by the fickle breeze. I walked briskly homewards, meditating with some amusement on the visitor's declamation on the purity of the Gael, suspecting that her opinion was based not so much on her own perception as on a superficial acquaintance with the excessive prudery of a Gaelic dictionary (which is so chaste that it gives only the alternate letters of any word that might be thought improper!). The remark had undoubtedly been offered in extenuation of the strange obsession of Janet's sister, Grace, whose story Janet had just been telling to the visitor.

Grace, even as a young girl, had never been particularly bright, and at fifteen she had 'got herself into trouble'. When she was fifty, Grace had suffered a slight stroke which, though not affecting her general health in any way, had left her with a fitful stammer and with an inexplicable aversion to the fly buttons on men's trousers. Her brothers began to find that if they left their trousers in the kitchen to dry overnight, when they came to put them on in the morning the fly buttons would all have been removed and the flies securely sewn up with strong thread. During the summer months when Janet took in boarders Grace's affliction had proved very embarrassing for the family and though they had kept a strict eye on her whenever male boarders came with wet clothes to be dried, she had on more than one occasion successfully eluded their vigilance. When Grace was sixty she had suffered yet another stroke which, though still not affecting her general health, had completely deprived her of the power of speech and, to the dismay of the family, had intensified her passion for correcting male attire. Her brothers now found it necessary to hide their trousers when they retired to bed because she would stealthily enter their rooms whilst they were asleep and appropriate any she could. The moment a male tourist entered the house Grace would fix the offending fly with a fierce stare, her fingers would hover above the scissors on their hook, and she would have to be strenuously dissuaded from following him up the stairs to his room, snapping the scissors anticipatorily. As Janet had confided to me, the only relief the family had was in knowing that she waited until the men had taken off their trousers before she 'Dis-Graced' them. Now Grace was nearing seventy. 'And dear knows what will happen if she has another stroke,' Janet had lamented. 'I can see us havin' to stop takin' in boarders altogether.' I suggested she should take only men who wear the kilt. 'No, no,' Janet had shaken her head dubiously. 'Maybe we'd better not risk that.' Comic as it seemed the problem was certainly a serious one for Janet and she had all my sympathy.

Around mid-day the following day the prolonged bellowing of a horn summoned me from my work. As a general rule I patronized the vans very little, begrudging the time I had to spend awaiting my turn. I could go to the village shop and get what I wanted in a quarter of the time and still be able to linger for a pleasant chat, but for some perishables and some of the more sophisticated items, like fruit juice and cream crackers, I had to rely on the vans.

'Did you hear why the van driver turned back last night?' I asked as I joined up with a group of crofters who, with rolled-up sacks under their arms, were already converging on the van and its inevitable entourage of scavenging gulls.

'Aye, poor man. It wasn't the dance at all he went back for. No, when he got to the top of the village he found he hadn't a dram to see him through the rest of the night, and he had such a thirst on him he just felt he couldn't wait another minute, so he turned straight back. He said he knew we'd all understand. Right enough, some was sayin' last night they'd be after reportin' him to the manager, but then they thought it was the dance he'd gone to. Ach, but you cannot hold a man's thirst against him.'

The wherewithal for a Hebridean to indulge his thirst seems to be always available, no matter how unremunerative his regular occupation may appear to be. I cannot explain why it should be so; I can only accept the fact that it is.

'Next for shavin'!' The gamekeeper's wife stepped down from the van and called out jovially as she stowed loaves and groceries into her sack and heaved it on to her shoulder. Whenever a Bruachite finished buying at a van it was the custom to call out wittily, 'Next for shavin'.' The phrase had been called out by every crofter at every van I had ever waited upon throughout the years and it had never failed to bring a chuckle from the audience; the Bruachites venerated age even in their jokes.

It was Old Murdoch's turn next. Though Murdoch lived with his sisters he did all the shopping because, he maintained, his sisters were too vague about the value of the different coins. Today Murdoch had been selling cattle and when he came to pay for his groceries he opened a purse well stuffed with notes. He was having, as Murdoch was invariably having, some tetchy argument with the van driver about the price of something he had bought and as he had no pipe handy to gesticulate with he used his open purse. A curious gull flew low over the van: in the next moment I realized that the word 'shit' can be onomatopoeic. The waiting crofters shrieked and fell back with laughter and Murdoch stared at his open purse with horror and disgust. It was the first time in my life I had seen a Gael look at money in such a way.

'That bloody gull's spilled into my poc!' he spluttered as though doubting the evidence of his own eyes.

We were all helpless with laughter and Murdoch, seeing himself as the chief entertainer, gallantly played up. He shook his fist at the gull; he danced about with rage. He gave every feather of the bird its full pedigree before he minced away holding his bulging purse at arm's length in front of him as apprehensively as though it had been a shovel full of hot coals. Altogether the scene was one of the funniest I have ever witnessed and when my own turn at the van came I had great difficulty in composing my features ready to make the serious complaint which was my main reason for wishing to see the driver.

In the Hebrides, where in the smaller village shops stocks are inclined to be slow moving, purchases might prove on occasion to be very unappetizing, sometimes inedibly so. In fact I had more than once been enabled to fulfil a life-long ambition to accept the printed invitation enclosed in each box of chocolates to 'return with this slip in case of complaint'. Generally speaking, one could understand and excuse, but the van driver had sold me mouldy bread and for this I could see no excuse at all. Admittedly mould grew prolifically in Bruach; so much so that one almost caught oneself pulling up one's sleeve to examine what was only a dark smudge on one's arm, but the bread I had bought was supposed to be fresh and it had been wrapped bread. Normally I baked my own, but a new cooker was in process of being installed in my kitchen—Hector and Erchy had between them undertaken the task, but with Hector mislaying 'tsings' and Erchy anticipating Jeannac's wedding, progress had been slow. The lack of a cooking stove had necessitated my buying bread temporarily and the first week I had got it fresh from the van, or so I had thought until I had taken off the wrapper and found it to be liberally spotted with mould. The following week when I had attended the van I had complained bitterly to the driver and threatened to report the matter unless he ensured that he sold me an uncontaminated loaf.

'How am I to tell whether a loaf's mouldy or not when it's all sealed up in a wrapper?' he had demanded pettishly.

'I don't make the damty stuff.'

'Well then, you'll just have to unwrap the loaf and examine it before you sell it to me,' I had insisted.

Ungraciously he had yielded and I had rejected about half his complement of loaves on the grounds of staleness or their resemblance to charred rubber before I was satisfied with the one I bought. However, when I came to cut a slice for my breakfast the next morning there was mould all the way through it.

Now, full of righteous indignation I stepped up to the van and glaring coldly at the driver reminded him of my complaint of the previous week and detailed unsparingly to him how, the very next morning, the loaf had been cut and found to be full of mould.

The driver made a pretence of listening earnestly and then returned my glare with an equally irate one.

'I'm damty glad it was mouldy then,' he said astonishingly.

I was thoroughly shaken. 'What did you say?'

'I said I'm damty glad it was mouldy. God! But that's funny,' he said, bursting into laughter. 'All that trouble you put me up to last week and all your greetin' and grumblin' and then you go and pick out a mouldy loaf for yourself.'

The van driver had the most infectious laugh in the world and it was a very merry shopping expedition for everyone that day.

Morag was waiting her turn when I stepped down. 'You're comin' to Jeannac's weddin' party tonight?' she asked, adding quickly, 'If you're spared.'

'Yes, of course,' I replied.

Jeannac and her husband had been married quietly a day or two previously on the mainland but now they had returned to have a proper wedding celebration at home.

'You mind when we were invited to her sister's weddin' two or three years back?' said Morag. 'It was on a Friday and they were boastin' that their weddin' cake weighed ten pounds, and the very next Friday they were boastin' the same about their baby, and you were that put out about it.'

I remembered it all very well. At the time I had been fairly new to Bruach and when the news of the birth of the baby had come so soon after the wedding I had been shocked indeed. Several months later when Morag and I had been collecting for some charity or other we had called at the house of the newlyweds. The baby had been crawling by then and such a delightful, bonny child was it that I was soon cuddling it and bouncing it on my knee. As we were coming away from the house I had observed to Morag that it was a lovely baby. 'Yes,' she had replied, 'but do you mind when you first heard it had come you said the couple should have been whipped?'

'Oh no!' I had at first protested, but the faint suspicion that I might once have been so intolerant as to have made such a remark grew into a positive recollection. I had felt thoroughly ashamed of myself.

'Yes, you did, mo ghaoil,' Morag had asserted. 'And I've never forgotten the look on your face when you said it.'

I have long since grown accustomed to 'God's wedding presents' being bestowed a little prematurely but there have been times in the wakeful hours of the night when I have wondered just what that wise old woman saw in my face that day.

The van's being delayed until the day of the wedding party had given me rather a rush of work. I had left Erchy putting the finishing touches to the new stove and there would, in addition to my ordinary chores, be the cleaning up of the kitchen afterwards. Intent on planning how best to accomplish everything I had to do, I was hurrying home when Peter jumped suddenly over the stone dyke from his croft with a gun under his arm. His appearance gave me a momentary fright but he dropped the gun abruptly, spat on his hand, rubbed it vigorously up and down his jacket, and offered it to me in greeting.

'Any luck with the rabbits, Peter?' I asked with a cautious glance at his abandoned gun which in places was bound with string and pieces of wire and looked as though it might prove more lethal to its handler than to any target.

'Yes, Miss,' he struggled breathlessly to tell me. 'One and a half.' His struggle for words was emphasized by the fact that his cap kept wriggling about on his head as he spoke.

'Jolly good,' I complimented him. 'But what happened to the other half?' (envisaging half a rabbit running back to its hole).

'He's no there when I go get he's, so I leave he's there.'

He lifted his cap, recaptured hastily the two moribund but not completely inert fish which escaped from it, replaced them and pulled his cap down more firmly on his head, leaving their tails hanging over his forehead in an animated fringe.

'Those will make a nice dinner for you and your mother, won't they?' I told him.

'Yes, Miss, I'm away to toast she's,' he said, retrieving his gun.

I was delighted to see smoke coming from the kitchen chimney of my cottage and when I pushed open the door Erchy, looking very glum for Erchy, was standing back speculatively.

'Wonderful!' I remarked with a contented smile.

'Aye, it's no so bad.'

'It's splendid,' I insisted, 'and the chimney seems to be drawing perfectly.' I lit the small gas ring and put on the kettle. 'You'll take a cup of coffee before you go?'

'Aye, thank you.'

'You do sound gloomy,' I told him. 'What's the matter? Disappointed because you didn't get away to the dance last night?'

'No indeed, I'm no disappointed about that at all.'

'Well, you're not like yourself,' I said.

'I don't feel like myself then.'

'You mean you're not feeling well?'

'Ach, I'm fine. I just don't feel like myself.'

I gave him a cup of coffee and put on the table some biscuits and cheese, and waited for the confidence which I knew was on its way.

'It's funny,' said Erchy, after a sip or two of coffee. 'I believe I must have been in love with Jeannac.'

'Jeannac? The Jeannac who got married on Wednesday?'

'Aye. I must have been in love with her, or why else would I feel so bad at her marryin' another man?'

I could only stare at him in speechless sympathy and wonder how much he was suffering.

'It was the same when Marjac got married. I felt just as bad then, so I knew I must have loved her,' he told me.

'But, didn't you realize before either of them married that you were in love with them?' I asked him.

'No, that's my trouble. I always have to wait for them to get married before I can tell. If I feel bad on their weddin' day then I know I was in love with them. If I don't feel bad I know I wasn't,' he said miserably.

His complaint, I thought, constituted the best recipe for remaining a bachelor that I had ever heard but Erchy was much too serious on the subject for me to dare any comment. I tried to take his mind off his sufferings.

'I suppose they've stocked up well with whisky for the party tonight?' I said.

'They stocked up well. They got seven bottles the other night and they thought they'd have a wee drink to start off with and before the night was through they'd finished the seven. I was there myself. Adam's havin' to go in to the pub on his motor bike to get some this evenin'.' He brightened considerably and by the time he had embarked on his second cup of coffee and reinspected the burning of the stove he was practically his normal self again. 'This coffee's good,' he approved. 'I don't rightly care much for coffee, but I like this stuff you make. Those pilgrims gave me a cup of coffee when I was in sortin' a chair for them the other day and it tasted no better than singed water.' He accepted a third cup and then decided he must go home and 'take his potatoes' (his dinner). 'I'll see you tonight,' he told me as he went.

'Yes,' I replied meaningly, 'probably in triplicate if past functions are anything to judge by.'

About ten minutes after he had left he was back again. 'Here, come and see a sight,' he commanded.

The afternoon sun was still shining brightly but within the hour it would be snugging itself down for the night behind the humped shapes of Rhuna and the outer islands, and I had a great deal to do before it got properly dark. I demanded to know if the sight were really worth my taking time off to see.

'I doubt you'll never see the like again,' promised Erchy. 'I've never seen it before anyway.'

He led me in the direction of Murdoch's cottage and how I wished when we got there that I had taken my camera with me. Murdoch, who by turns was irascible, obstreperous, rhetorical and benign, was born to be a clown. If there was a situation in which he was involved it would inevitably become a comic one. He sat there now in his garden on an upturned pail watching with morosely unswerving eyes about twenty dripping one-pound and five-pound notes which were pinned with safety pins to his clothes line.

'God!' murmured Erchy appreciatively, 'the old bodach's washed the lot of it.'

When I arrived for the wedding party at Jeannac's house the guests were already overflowing the kitchen and 'the room' and were sitting happily on the stairs right up to the tiny landing. For all I knew there may have been more in the bedrooms. The heat inside hit one like a poultice though cold breaths of frost panted in through the wide-open door. I managed to insinuate myself into a corner of the kitchen where someone handed me a glass of sherry and a piece of crumbled cake. Everyone was talking and laughing happily and strangely enough no one appeared to be more than moderately intoxicated. Sandy Beag called that we ought to be dancing and clutching the reluctant Jeannac he started to jig, kicking his feet behind him but he was made to desist after nearly de-skirting one or two of the black-draped old women who were standing near.

'Here, take her, Ian,' Sandy Beag pushed the bride towards her groom who was leaning pallidly against the dresser.

The announcement of the engagement of Jeannac and Ian had hit the village with startling suddenness and no matter who I met during the intervening weeks before the wedding day the question 'Why is Jeannac marrying Ian?' was always one of the first to be asked. The Bruachites were great diagnosticians. In sickness, whether of animals or humans, the symptoms were discussed profoundly and the ailment diagnosed before the arrival of the vet or the doctor. The symptoms of a forthcoming wedding were discussed in much the same way, for though addicted to romantic fiction the crofters were sceptical of romance in their own lives and they liked to have some incontrovertible reason to offer for any impending marriage. The engagement of the vet brought the comment, 'Well, right enough he's got to have someone to answer the telephone for him,' while another marriage, an obviously incompatible union, was excused because 'since his mother's died his sister's afraid to sleep by herself and they can't afford a girl to share her bed.' However, I had heard no plausible reason advanced for Jeannac's acceptance of Ian. Jeannac was strikingly good looking, intelligent and financially secure, and looking across at her now, glowingly happy beside the sleazy Ian, I wondered more than ever why she had chosen him. I said so out loud to Old Murdoch and Morag, who were standing close beside me.

'Ach, well, Miss Peckwitt,' Old Murdoch began with a slightly apologetic air, 'a woman comes to a certain stage just like a salmon at the back end that will jump at a piece of old rag, and then she'll take anythin' at all.'

'But Jeannac's not old,' I protested, turning to Morag for confirmation. 'Surely you don't think it's a case of last chance with Jeannac?'

'No,' she admitted, 'I dunna believe it's that at all, but I'm hearin' he made a song for her, though what was in it she never told a soul, and then she made a song back for him and the next everybody knew they was plannin' to get married.'

'Did you hear how the wedding went off?' I asked.

'Ach, it was quiet just. Just the two of them and Johnny and Elspeth, though I did hear that Johnny was so keen not to lose the ring he put it on his own little finger and when he came to hand it to the bridegroom it had got stuck. He was after havin' a great struggle with it, Elspeth said, and indeed at one time she thought Ian would be after marryin' Johnny with the way it was.'

More and more people were packing into the house and a good deal of drink was being spilled on dresses and suits and on the floor as we were jostled against one another. I was thinking how much more pleasant it might have been if the party had taken place in the summer so that the guests could perhaps have taken their refreshments outside and conversed or danced without too much discomfort.

'Here,' said Erchy, threading his way towards us with an open bottle of whisky. 'You're lookin' miserable. Fill up your glass, there'll be plenty more when Angus gets back.'

'I'm not miserable,' I denied, lifting my still half-full glass out of reach of the threatening bottle. 'But Erchy,' I asked him. 'Tell me will you why Bruach people always choose the winter time for their weddings?'

Erchy stared me firmly in the eye. 'Because the nights are longer,' he replied with unflinching candour.

'What's happened to Angus?' asked Morag.

'They're wonderin' that themselves,' replied Erchy. 'He went off on Adam's motor bike to get some more drinks about three hours ago and he said he'd be back within the hour, and he's no back yet.' He wandered away again, still proffering the bottle indiscriminately.

'I didn't know Angus could ride a motor bike,' I murmured to Morag.

'I don't believe he can,' she said, 'but he's gone off on it just the same. Somebody had to go, they said, and Adam's crinkled his back and canna' stand up on his legs.'

'I should jolly well think they would be wondering what has happened to him in that case,' I said with an anxious glance in the direction of Angus's mother. 'He might have had a spill.'

'Ach, if that lad has a spill he'll make sure he chooses a soft spot,' said Morag lightly.

One of the highlights of the evening was to be the reading of the congratulatory telegrams without which no Highland wedding would really be complete. After much hilarious discussion it was decided to wait to read them until Angus had returned so that he should not miss the fun. Since attending my first wedding in Bruach I had become inured to hearing the youth of the village composing bawdy messages to send to their friends when they got married. In the last few years Hebridean post offices have become much less easy-going than they used to be in their attitude to the sending of such messages and there had been bitter complaints this time that two of the verses composed for the congratulatory telegrams had been refused for transmission on the grounds of their being too coarse. Dollac, who was not only beautiful but also as happy natured a girl as I have ever met, was particularly adept at such compositions and when the subject came up she was loud in her condemnation of the post office.

'Oh come,' I pleaded, 'they must have been pretty bad if the post office refused them.'

'Indeed they were no bad at all. I've sent worse. They're gettin' so particular nowadays it won't be worth while spendin' our money on them.'

'Tell Miss Peckwitt what was in yours,' urged Morag, with a sly smile.

'Yes, go on, tell me,' I encouraged.

Dollac giggled. 'May your honeymoon be like our dining-room table—four legs and no drawers,' she quoted unblushingly.

'And the other one?'

'Ach, that was just:

Ian, Ian, don't be shy,
Put out the light and have a damn good try.'

'What's wrong with those, I'd like to know?' demanded Morag indignantly. 'They must have nasty minds those telegraph fellows.'

'They're no worse than I sent my cousin when he got married,' said Dollac, 'and they took that one all right.'

'What did you have to say then?' I pressed, conscious of a sneaking admiration.

'Two little pillows edged with lace,
Two little people face to face,
And everything in its proper place,'

she recited amidst shrieks of female laughter.

At this moment Angus flung himself sulkily through the door and plonked down some bottles emphatically on the table.

'Why Angus, what on earth has been keepin' you back?' asked his mother.

'Those bloody pollis, that's what,' Angus retorted with seething resentment.

A strained hush fell over the kitchen. 'You mean you're after bein' caught?' his mother whispered.

'Caught? No, but I had a lucky escape.' He ladled himself a drink of water and swallowed two or three times before pouring the rest back into the pail. 'What happened was I was just comin' out of the bar when I sees those two pollis passin' in their car. They sees me and they stops. "Where are you away to?" they asks me, quite friendly. "I'm away home," I tells them, "whenever I can get. I've just been gettin' the drinks for my sister's weddin' party." "And how are you gettin' home," they asks me. Well I couldn't tell them I had the motor bike because I have no driving licence and anyway Adam has no insurance for his bike. "There's a fellow goin' that way says he would give me a lift," I says. They asked me who it was so I told them the only name I could think of. "Ach," they says, "you'll wait all night for him, he left over an hour ago. Come on and we'll give you a lift with us." I was swearin' to myself I can tell you. "Are you goin' to Bruach?" I asks them. "Not all the way," they says, "but a good part of it. Come on and jump in." I knew if I didn't go with them then they'd guess somethin' and start lookin' around. So I just didn't look at Adam's motor bike and I got into the car with them and they took me as far as Sheehan. Indeed at one time I thought the buggers were goin' to take me farther. When they stopped, I got out and as soon as they was out of sight I hid the bottles in the ditch and started walkin' back again to the pub for I didn't want the bike to be found there. When I got there the pollis car was still not back from Sheehan. Hell! I thought, what do I do now? So what I did was to get on the bike and start off, for by this time it was dark and every time I saw a pair of headlights comin' towards me I had to jump off and fling myself and the bike into the ditch and lie flat. I'm wet through. I could have murdered those bloody pollis, I can tell you.'

Relief spread over everyone's face at the successful outcome of Angus's escapade and at the sight of the full bottles on the table. The party rapidly became noisier and distinctly less pleasant so far as I was concerned. The male Bruachites firmly believe that they must get drunk before they can enjoy themselves, and the women, who seemed to find the men too inhibited unless they were drunk, encouraged them in their belief.

In 'the room' a gramophone began to contribute to the general cacophony and Morag drew me through there to listen to records of Gaelic songs. They found a record of 'Loch Lomond' which they put on for me because it was in English, though it was little more than a tuneless whisper.

'That record is nearly worn out,' I said to Morag.

'Yes,' she rejoined, 'but it's a very old tune, isn't it?'

Janet, looking very merry and bright, beckoned us into the kitchen where tea was being prepared and we inched our way through, passing Erchy, who was sprawled on a bench beside Sadie, a young girl from a neighbouring village. Sadie was full-bosomed, strong and possessed of gypsy-like good looks and Erchy was proposing marriage to her with sleepy earnestness. 'An' I'll make you a good . . . good husband,' he was saying. '. . . An' I'll work . . . work hard. . . .'

I smiled to myself recalling the autumn day when I had met Erchy, looking very harassed, making for his home at the double, his scythe over his shoulder. Only a short time previously I had seen him scything the corn on his croft so I called out to him, teasingly, that he was leaving off too early.

'Indeed it's no that at all,' he had replied breathlessly. 'But that Sadie and her friend is down there in the grass shoutin' to me and I'm damty feart they'll have the trousers off me if I stay much longer on my own. I'm away to get my mother to work beside me.'

'An I'll look after all the bairns . . .' he was saying now, as he patted her knee with befuddled repetition.

We reached the relative quiet of the kitchen.

'Janet, what has happened to your visitor?' I asked. 'She should be here tonight, shouldn't she?'

'Indeed, mo ghaoil, she's away to her bed long ago.' Our eyes met and we exchanged a grin of understanding. 'Aye,' Janet added, smiling, 'she's gone to bed with a Gaelic dictionary.'

Johnny, coming in to replenish glasses, overheard the remark. 'That's a damty funny thing for a woman to want to go to bed with,' he commented.

By midnight the house was thick with tobacco fumes and resonant with song and laughter, shrieks and shrill argument. Cups were being hooked and as quickly unhooked from dresser shelves as a chorus of steaming kettles was whisked from the stove to wash dishes or to brew tea and then to be refilled for yet more tea. My head had begun to throb with the heat and I felt I could unobtrusively slip away. Outside, revived by the frosty air, I loitered for a few moments looking through the windows, curtained only by condensation, at the happy throng within. The old men were singing tranquilly, with half-closed eyes, their joined hands lifting and falling to the beat of the tune. The old women chattered animatedly. The young people teased one another and giggled disproportionately. On the bench Erchy was still sprawled, still making the same earnest proposals, still patting a knee—but it was a different girl!

XII. *The Christmas Party*

LONG AFTER THE WAVERING 'Vs' of geese had passed over on their way south and advertisements in the national newspapers had begun to draw our attention to the ordering of Christmas cards, some of us in Bruach were still making hay, pulling with numb fingers the frosty, wet patches from cocks which had taken in the wet and scattering it to dry on days of intermittent and glacial sunshine. Hallowe'en, which normally sees the end of the harvest, overtook us and still there was hay to be gathered in. Only the children exulted, Hallowe'en being the one day in the year which they could really call their own. From about mid-October they were preparing for it, designing for themselves masks of painted cardboard on which they sewed fearsome quantities of unwashed fleece, and rooting under beds and in lofts for discarded garments so as to further disguise them-

243

selves. The clothes they unearthed were almost invariably black and reeking of mildew or manure depending upon where they had been stored and as soon as it was dark on Hallowe'en, the children arrayed in their masks and stumbling about in voluminous skirts or rolled-up trousers and looking more like guys for a bonfire than revellers, banded together to visit each house in turn. There, not speaking or unmasking until their identities had been guessed correctly, they waited in musty groups to receive an apple or a sixpence before rushing off on their rounds. Once all the houses had been visited and perhaps some apple-dunking indulged in at one or two of the more cordial homes, the children threw away their masks, abandoned their old clothes beside the road for collection later and embarked on the really exciting business of the evening.

It was a strictly honoured tradition in Bruach that at Hallowe'en nothing is ever 'stolen'. If spades or forks disappeared from a shed overnight, or a wheelbarrow from a byre, it was just part of the fun. If you were unlucky enough or lazy enough to have potatoes still in the ground and you found them uprooted and scattered over the croft, or if a hay rake disappeared completely because the children could not remember what, in their excitement, they had done with it, then it was 'Ach well, we was all young once'. A wheelbarrow or a cart might suffer damage during its nocturnal journey, but what else could you expect? 'It was too heavy for the children to manage of course.' Bruach did not have child delinquents. They were allowed to get it all out of their system in one glorious Hallowe'en spree.

As a result of the late harvest many implements had not been stored away for the winter and the revellers, sometimes reinforced by their elders, made the most of their opportunities. I awoke next morning to find my garden gate had been replaced by Peter's harrows and that Yawn's barrow was hidden beneath a pile of discarded clothes in my byre. When I set out to locate the gate, which the smiling grocer had discovered at the back of his 'wee hoosie', I was joined by many of the neighbours, all grumbling good-naturedly as they searched out their belongings in all sorts of unexpected places. In company with them I found myself staring stupidly at a colourful array of ladies' underwear pegged out on the clothes-line at the bachelor home of Farquhar until I recognized it as some of my own which I had forgotten to take in the previous night. By midday, everyone seemed to have reclaimed his property and even the most irascible sufferer had been soothed by the laughter of his neighbours. Only Sheena, who had made the mistake of sending the children away without reward or invitation to enter, because the previous year they had managed to secrete a live hedgehog in her bed, still nursed a grievance, for the children had repaid her churlishness by climbing on to the roof of her cottage and placing a sod on top of the chimney.

'Me and Peter was sittin' in the kitchen and I was readin' the paper to him when the smoke started to come down the chimbley as though it was on the funnel of a ship we was,' she told me, her red-rimmed eyes still moist with indignation. 'Of course it's no a right chimbley at the best of times but, "Peter," I says, "we must get some heather up here tomorrow," I says. Mercy!, but the smoke got that thick I can tell you I was takin' bites out of it.' She bit the air demonstratively. ' "Peter," I tells him, "for the dear Lord's sake open up that door for fear we'll be like the kippers with the smoke." Peter goes to open the door. "It's stuck, cailleach," he tells me. "Never!" says I, not believin' what he was sayin', but when I tried would it open it was stuck right enough. "Help!" I shouts, for by this time me and Peter is coughin' our stomachs near into our throats. "Help!" I calls again, though who would be after hearin' me I'd not be knowin'. Then I hears them childrens laughin' outside. "Help! Open the door for us, childrens," I calls to them, but they just laughs and shouts back at me and mocks me and they bide their time till they think we've had enough before they cut the string that's tyin' the door and scramble away. Peter and me, we just fell outside with the coughin' we was doin', and there in the moonlight Peter points up and he says to me, "There's no smoke comin' from the chimbley, cailleach," and I looks and I see what's happened for fine I remember the boys doin' it when I was young. "You get up on that roof right away, Peter," I tells him, "and get that sod off the chimbley." He went up, tremblin' and shiverin', for he has no head for the heights, mo ghaoil, and I was shiverin' myself with the cold before I was able to go back inside again, and this mornin' I see my bed's all yellow with the stain of it.' Sheena sighed noisily and shook her head over the brutal treatment she had received.

After Hallowe'en was over, there was nothing for the

children to look forward to except the spectacle of their elders getting drunk at New Year, which they considered vastly amusing. Christmas, as I had soon found, was ignored completely. The only time I can recall feeling lonely was when I had gone for a walk on my first Christmas morning in Bruach and had gaily wished everyone a 'Happy Christmas'. Not one of the people I met had returned my greeting with a trace of enthusiasm, their response being an embarrassed 'Yes, it's a nice day,' as though I had said something out of place. I learned later that though one religious sect did in fact condemn the celebration of Christmas, most of my neighbours had not returned my greeting simply because the unexpectedness of it had left them at a loss for a conventional reply.

It seemed to me that a children's party at Christmas would be a good idea and I set about planning one. My motives, I regret to say, were not entirely unselfish, for I love the tinsel and glitter and the festivities and bustle that go with Christmas, and a children's party would provide the excuse for plenty of it and so do much to enliven the day for me. The cottage was far too small for entertaining more than one or two people at a time but I had now had built a new shed of corrugated iron with a concrete floor. Assessing with Dollac and her friends the suitability of the shed for a party, it emerged that it was a pity there was to be only a celebration for the children.

'We could have a grand dance here,' said Dollac, and began humming as she danced across the floor.

'I don't see why we shouldn't put on a pantomime in

this village,' I said without much seriousness.

'A what?'

'A pantomime.'

'What's a pantomime?' They turned to me with faces that were both puzzled and amused.

'Oh, you know what I mean,' I said, thinking there was probably an obscure Gaelic word for pantomime. 'Plays like *Cinderella* and *Mother Goose* and *Aladdin.*'

'Who did you say? Cinderella? Mother of Goose? What are they? What was a lad in?'

I found it difficult to accept that they really had never heard of any of them. 'Well,' I began to explain. 'You know the story of Cinderella, don't you? The poor little girl with the two ugly sisters and the fairy godmother. . . .' Their expressions were revealingly blank. So I told them the story, adding that in pantomime the male parts, except for the dastardly villains, were usually played by females and that the comic female parts were usually played by men. They thought it a splendid idea and it was decided there and then that we would celebrate Christmas, first by having a children's party to be followed by a pantomime at which the children could be present and then, after the children had gone home, by a dance for adults. The children were obviously delighted at the prospect: the adolescents greeted the news of the pantomime and dance with restrained enthusiasm and the older people, after praising me for my generosity, predicting great success for each of the entertainments planned and fervidly assuring me of their intention to be present, retired into their cocoons of Calvinism and waited to see what everyone else would do about the whole affair. Remembering the fiasco of the pilgrims' party I knew that I too must wait and see.

I wrote a pantomime that I thought would amuse the village, which meant that I could unashamedly use all the chestnuts I had ever heard. I also, perhaps a little cruelly, gave one or two members of the cast the opportunity of openly criticizing my early attempts at crofting, which I knew had caused much humorous comment locally. Buttons' haircut was supposed to look 'as though Miss Peckwitt had been at it with a scythe'. A rickety chair was to collapse 'like a Peckwitt hay-cock'. My intention was to try to convey to them that I accepted their criticism ruefully but as well deserved, but the cast defeated me by courteously ignoring such lines, even when the text did not make sense without them. To my surprise rehearsals were not only well attended but were enormous fun and those few weeks leading up to Christmas were, I think, the most hilarious I have ever spent in my life. On three or four nights of every week we assembled at the cottage to read our lines and no one, I think, was serious for a single moment of the time. The roadman and the shepherd capered through the parts of the ugly sisters lustily. Erchy, as the stepfather, was impressive when he could remember not to read out all the stage directions with his speeches; he was an absolute riot when he forgot. The postman, who was playing Buttons, used to come in the middle of his round, sling his half-empty mailbag into a corner of the hall and, with his mobile face creased in anticipation and his eyes shining conspiratorially, read over his part with prickly voiced diffidence. The postman's presence was vital, for he was also providing the melodeon music for the chorus to dance to until we could get suitable records.

'What about the mails?' I asked him one time.

'Ach, they know where I am,' he replied with supreme indifference.

I tried to insist that rehearsals should cease at midnight but the Bruachites, who regard midnight as an hour to begin enjoying oneself, had other ideas. They would put back my clock while I was out of the room or put back their watches and swear my clock was fast so that more often than not it was two or perhaps four o'clock in the morning before I could seek my bed and then only because the pressure lamp had defiantly put an end to proceedings by running out of paraffin. As Christmas bore down upon us excitement mounted visibly, more particularly among the children from whom I had begun to receive adoring looks as soon as the party had been announced. 'Tea-parties' became a new game and Fiona, who had been taken by Behag and Morag for a day out on the mainland and who had, as a matter of course, given them the slip, had excelled herself by being discovered in the comparatively urban graveyard engrossed in a game of 'tea-parties' with a grave for a table for which she had collected a bevy of decorative urns and jars from the surrounding graves.

A great disappointment for me was that a box of decorations which I had ordered failed to arrive and two days before Christmas Eve I was faced with the prospect not only of baking all the fancy cakes needed for the party and for the light refreshments at the dance but also with the decorating of a bare corrugated iron shed to which, by hook or by crook, I was determined to give a festive appearance. The solution came unexpectedly when Behag and Morag, who had not been able to finish their shopping on the mainland because of having to search for Fiona, asked me if I would look after the child for the day whilst they went off on their own. I visualized myself spending Christmas Day in bed recuperating from twelve hours with Fiona, but she had not been in the house for more than half an hour before she was demanding paints. I was so relieved she had chosen such an innocuous way of passing the time that I hastened to indulge her.

'You can paint some Christmas decorations for me,' I said, giving her some sheets of thick paper and a particularly robust brush. I went back to my baking.

'I'm needin' more paper,' Fiona ordered briskly.

I rummaged in the cupboard and found more paper which she had covered with splodges of paint almost before I could return to my bowl. It was her incessant demands for paper that gave me the inspiration. I brought out a toilet roll.

'You can paint the whole length of that,' I told her firmly. 'Use lots of bright colours and don't you dare ask for more paper until you've painted every bit of it.' Even Fiona was momentarily daunted by the task I had set her but determinedly she set to work, singing with preoccupied tunelessness to herself as she daubed her way along the whole length of the roll. The table top was covered in plastic; Fiona was enveloped in an old overall; there was plenty of paint—and toilet rolls. I carried on blissfully with my cooking and when I could spare a few minutes from it Fiona and I cut up the daubed paper into decorative garlands which we later carried out to the shed. When Hector came to collect his daughter we showed him the results of her artistic skill which the child, as though ashamed of my own rapture, dismissed with adult coolness as being 'no bad at all'. Hector immediately volunteered to come next day and hang them for me and with uncharacteristic fidelity he came, bringing a curious Erchy along with him. They were each carrying big bundles of holly and ivy. I had run out of flour and was getting ready to go over to Sarah's to borrow some when the two men arrived so I left them to their work, telling them that if I was not back by the time they had finished they could make themselves a cup of tea and help themselves to scones. The kitchen was luxuriant with trays of tarts and cakes and buns of every kind but, I warned, they were strictly party fare.

'My, but they make my teeths water,' said Erchy, looking covetously about him. 'I believe I could eat the lot.'

'You must promise not to eat anything but the scones,' I told them, and they promised cheerfully.

Before I closed the door I turned to look back at the kitchen, making sure that everything was safely stacked and that I had not left anything in the oven. The sight gave me a great deal of pleasure. On the dresser, already gay with its poppy and blue china, were three trays of sponge cakes waiting to be crowned with a whirl of cream. Éclair cases ready to be filled and iced were piled on the top of the trolly: cream horns wanting their insides stoked with jam and cream covered the bottom. Beside the stove a large sponge cake, roughly shaped like a boat waited to receive its cargo of children's names in coloured letters. On the kitchen table, with its black and white chequered plastic top, reposed trays of blackcurrant and lemon curd tarts, making a colourful centrepiece. My own teeths began to water and I shut the door firmly.

When I called, Sarah was herself preparing to bake girdle scones, while Flora watched impassively. 'Surely, mo ghaoil, but I've plenty of flour,' Sarah assured me as she swung the girdle to one side and pushed the whispering kettle on to the peats. 'Just sit now and rest a bitty while I make a wee strupak.'

I had hoped that she would be busy about the sheds and that I should escape without having to wait for a strupak, but when I sat down I found I was glad to do so. Having spent the whole of the previous two days baking, I felt I was going to enjoy the sight of someone else doing some. Sarah spread a newspaper over the table and floured it liberally. My neighbours made wonderful girdle scones but despite repeated demonstrations I had never been able to achieve just the lightness and texture in my baking that they unfailingly achieved in theirs. Perhaps it was because I used a well-floured baking board to press out my scones instead of a well-floured newspaper. She reached down a small pudding basin from the dresser—another essential for baking good scones seemed to be the use of a too small bowl so that the flour could spill over when mixing began. She brought out a tin of cream of tartar and a tin of baking soda from the cupboard and then stopped in her tracks to peer with a puzzled frown about the kitchen. Several times I had thought I could hear the plaintive miaow of a cat but I had refrained from mentioning it, suspecting that it was quite possibly entombed beneath Flora's skirts and that if this were the case it would only be a matter of time before it burrowed its way out again. Sarah went into 'the room' and brought out a jug of sour milk which she set on the table.

'I can hear that cat somewhere,' she said, looking all round the kitchen again. She picked up the basin and went over to the large wallpaper-decorated barrel which stood beside the fireplace. As she lifted the lid a startled exclamation burst from her and an albino cat leaped on the rim of the barrel and then down to the floor where it sneezed, shook itself vigorously and revealed itself as tortoise-shell. 'Well,' said Sarah, 'so that's where he's been hidin' all this time; in my flour barrel.' She gave a little self-conscious chuckle, dipped the basin down into the flour barrel and began to mix her scones. The cat continued to miaow and rubbed itself against her boots.

'She seems glad to be out again,' I said.

'I expect the beast's hungry,' said Sarah. 'Dear knows how long he's been in there.'

I hurried home, clutching my bag of flour and salving my conscience by recalling some of the less hygienic practices of my neighbours. I could, I told myself, keep back the cakes baked with Sarah's flour and produce them only if and when everything else had been eaten. There was no sound of hammering or of voices when I reached the cottage and I went to the shed to see what was happening. The decorations were up and, betraying not the slightest sign of their humble origin, looked 'beautiful just'. The holly had been nailed in bunches along the walls: ivy cascaded from the roof. In one corner, a tub (an old salt-herring barrel) already filled with peat waited to receive the Christmas tree which was due to arrive the following evening. With a sigh of relief I closed the door. The silence everywhere coupled with the non-appearance of either Erchy or Hector made me wonder if they had already gone home and as I passed the kitchen window I glanced inside. The two men were sitting at either end of the kitchen table with cups of tea beside them. Their chins were resting on their left hands, their right hands held cigarettes from which they flicked the ash periodically into their gumboots. They were looking down at the checked table top with the dedicated air of keen chess players and neither noticed my presence outside the window. I waited a moment before announcing myself and saw Erchy push something a little along the table towards Hector. To my horror I saw it was a blackcurrant tart! Hector retaliated by pushing a lemon curd tart one square towards Erchy. I peered closer and suddenly divining the reason for their absorption I bounded inside.

'Hector and Erchy!' I upbraided them. 'What do you think you're doing with those tarts?'

They both looked up in pained surprise. 'Only playin'

draughts,' said Erchy mildly, as with a triumphant flourish he passed a blackcurrant tart over a lemon curd and drew the spoils towards him.

'But you promised not to touch them,' I reminded them petulantly as I hurried forward to retrieve my precious baking.

'We promised not to eat tsem and we haven't,' said Hector earnestly. 'Honest, we haven't touched a one.' He disentangled a couple of 'crowns' as he spoke, examining their jammy bottoms. 'Look!' he insisted, 'tsey're as good as new.'

I loaded the tarts back on to the trays, sourly ignoring their pleas to 'let's finish the game out'.

'Ach well, I near had him beat anyway,' said Erchy, getting up. 'My but those scones of yours was so light it was like bitin' into a cloud,' he added with awkward flattery.

'Indeed tsey was beautiful just,' supported Hector fulsomely. 'I was after sayin' to Erchy, if only we could eat our draughts when tse game was over, I wouldn't mind losin'.'

Early in the afternoon of Christmas Eve the tree arrived, a magnificent specimen generously contributed by the estate manager. Morag and Dollac were with me at the time helping me to put the finishing touches to the fancy cakes, and we all left off to go and see the tree installed in its barrel. Erchy, Hector and deaf Ruari who, though he claimed to be too old to be interested in such frivolities, was just as curious over the preparations as were the younger generation, had appointed themselves to escort the tree, and inevitably there was argument as to which branches must be cut off and whether the barrel was suitable and whether it was sufficiently stable, but at last they reached agreement and the tree stood gracefully awaiting our attention, its fresh resiny smell filling the shed.

I sniffed appreciatively and winked at Morag.

'Ruari!' scolded Morag loudly. 'You must send your dog out of here. He's throwin smells.'

'Aye, I got some new meal for him yesterday an' I don't believe it's agreein' with him right,' Ruari submitted by way of explanation when he had ordered the dog outside.

Morag and Dollac and I returned to the kitchen to finish our preparations there before starting to decorate the tree.

'Did I ever tell you?' asked Morag as she painstakingly halved cherries to top the cream cakes, 'I worked in a bakery once and I used to watch the baker decoratin' the cakes with halves of cherries just like I'm doin' now, but my fine fellow wouldn't bother himself to cut the cherries in half. Oh, no, he just would bite them in half.' I wondered fleetingly if she was suggesting she should do likewise and was immensely relieved when she continued, 'I've never eaten a cake with a cherry on the top since.' I debated whether to mention the cat in the flour barrel, but decided against it. I had already taken a bite of one of the cakes made from the flour and though I had come to the conclusion that the cat had been in the barrel for quite a long time, the cake was, I felt, far more palatable than, for instance, Sheena's shortbread.

Midnight had already chimed before we had finished the tree and the long tables which had been borrowed from the school canteen had been covered with wallpaper that had originally been intended for stage decoration but which, due to the non-arrival of the previously mentioned parcel, was to serve a dual purpose—once the children's tea was finished it would have to be whipped off and used for papering Cinderella's kitchen. There had been so many late nights since the hectic preparations for Christmas had begun and when I had managed to get an early night in the hope of catching up on some sleep it had resulted only in catching up on dreams, so I was utterly weary by the time Morag and Dollac, after repeated 'beautiful justs' as they surveyed the evening's work, departed by the light of a reluctant moon. It was still dark on Christmas morning when I began to lay the tables in the shed. As I carried out the plates of cakes and pastries, Rhuna emerged duskily across the water, its string of lamplit windows dim as tarnished tinsel against the brilliant flashes of the lighthouses. When the sun rose it was smudged and angry and with it wakened an aggressive wind that swept the rain in from the sea. Some of the children lived a good distance away from the village and I had promised to collect them in 'Joanna' if it was a nasty day. Accordingly, about four o'clock in the afternoon, I drove through the slatting rain to collect the first of my guests. Marjac, whose five children were all dodding about just inside the door, greeted me with shrill querulousness.

'What on earth am I to do with Shamus?' she demanded. 'He was out on the hill this mornin' and got his trousers soakin' wet so he had to put on his best ones. Now hasn't he caught himself on John Willy's harrows and torn the seat out of them.' Marjac darted back to her sewing machine and turned the handle savagely. 'I'm after makin' him a pair from one of my old skirts,' she said disgustedly. Shamus, a little shamefaced, went to the solid wood kerb in front of the fire and sat down, carefully arranging an old meal sack over his lower half. The rest of the children were ready and impatient to be off. 'There you are,' his mother flung the trousers at Shamus, and clutching at the sack he hurried away to 'the room' to put them on.

'Ian, did you wash your teeths like the nurse told you?' Marjac arrested another of her brood with the question just as he was about to slip through the door.

'No, I didn't yet,' Ian replied.

'Then if nurse sees you she'll ask you and be vexed with you,' his mother warned. 'She'll be at the party, won't she, Miss Peckwitt?' I nodded. 'Nurse says he's got bad teeths and she's given him a brush and some paste to try will he keep the rest from goin' too,' Marjac explained as Ian reached at the back of the dresser for his toothbrush, moistened it by dipping it into the kettle and proceeded to attack his teeth with as much energy as if he were attacking rusty iron with a file.

'What a good thing you were able to run up a pair of trousers for Shamus,' I complimented Marjac during a lull in the activity.

'Ach, I just threw them together out of my head,' she disclaimed.

Shamus came out from 'the room' looking a little perplexed. One trouser-leg was skin tight; the other hung loosely about his thigh. He looked beseechingly at his mother.

'It'll have to do,' she told him. 'Miss Peckwitt cannot wait here all day while I see to it.'

I might have offered to wait, but I doubted if there was much Marjac could do to the trousers except to cut down the wide leg to match the tight one and thus immobilize the mobile half also. The children packed themselves into the car, Shamus rather stiltedly, and I was soon decanting them into Morag's care and rushing away for the rest. By five o'clock all the children had arrived and were waiting tensely in the cottage for what was going to happen next. It is rare for even very young Gaelic children to betray excitement noisily and so it was a very decorous procession indeed which followed me to the shed. There, they seated themselves at the tables as they were directed, not scrambling for places but scolding one another in loud whispers whenever they detected signs of stupidity or slowness. When they were settled they regarded the heaped-up plates of delicacies with prim dignity. I insisted that everyone should begin with bread and butter or sandwiches and these they accepted demurely only when Morag and I pressed them to do so. We offered them cakes, for which they reached out cautious hands. Remembering their zest for school meals I found their apathy when confronted with my cooking dispiriting. I began to wonder if, not being accustomed to fancy cookery, they had not developed an appetite for it, but in view of their consumption of sweets, jam and biscuits, it seemed highly improbable. I knew there was nothing wrong with my cooking and every now and then I caught the gleam in their eyes as they stared along the length of the loaded tables. I signalled to Morag to come to the door with me and there I turned.

'Look, children,' I said. 'Morag and I must go and see to things in the kitchen but there's to be a competition and a shilling for the one who eats the most. Keep a check on one another and tell me when I come back and the winner will get a shilling and the next two sixpence each.'

They whispered meekly that they would and we left them sitting like jaded gourmands before the feast. The moment the door closed uproar began, and I heard it with satisfaction. We left them for half an hour and when we returned the tables looked as though they had been swept by a hurricane. Shyness and stiffness were completely gone and everyone was clamouring to tell us who had won the shilling.

'Johnny! Johnny's won,' they yelled. 'He had twenty-four cakes and four sandwiches.'

Johnny smiled angelically as he pocketed his shilling.

Shamus was one of the runners up, and one of the youngest children was the other, though we found that he had eaten only the cream centres out of four of his cakes and disposed of the rest under the table.

By eight o'clock the players were beginning to arrive for the pantomime and the 'stage', which was merely one end of the shed sketchily partitioned off and curtained, had to be set. Various helpers came, bringing old railway sleepers which they had collected from the shore and which they set up on old salt herring barrels to provide seating accommodation for the audience. The children, full, and tired after a series of games, were content to sit and watch preparations from the front stalls. Dollac, who naturally was playing Cinderella, rushed in, still wearing gumboots and an old mac, on her way back from taking the hill cows their evening feed. She had been caught in a hail shower and she looked so ravishing with her glowing cheeks and rippling black hair flecked with hailstones that it seemed ludicrous to attempt to make her more emphatic with stage makeup. The postman bustled in to become Buttons.

'That'll make some nice presents for the audience— when they get them,' he said meaningly, indicating the bulging mail bag behind the Christmas tree. 'See and put the postmistress on the back row all the same.'

The pantomime frolicked along from start to finish. The players forgot their lines but the audience knew the play at least as well as the actors (the script had been passed round the village like a best-selling book), so that there were no embarrassing intervals of silence. The chorus tripped through their dances with earnest efficiency, rigidly following the beat of the music even when the gramophone ran down and was wound up again with the record still playing. During rehearsals I had tried, unavailingly, to persuade them to smile as they danced, but tonight they appeared to have great difficulty in repressing their amusement, the obliging little postman having overcome their impassivity by placing himself on the front row ready to make faces at them whenever they appeared on the stage. The audience were enchanted.

'My, but I believe Dollac was as good as any of them fillum stars,' said Morag admiringly when the pantomime was over and the children had gone home. We were in the kitchen hurriedly cutting up more sandwiches, making more tea and replenishing the dishes of cakes, while everyone who could was throwing out or rearranging the herring barrels and sleepers to clear the floor for dancing.

'She'd make any film star I've ever seen look pretty sick,' I said.

'Indeed, yes,' agreed Behag, who had glamorized herself for the occasion by putting on a new dress which became her, and by powdering her face inexpertly so that she succeeded in looking mildewed. 'I was seein' in the paper a day or two ago that some fillum star had just taken her fifth husband.'

'She needs her bumps reading,' I observed dispassionately.

'She needs what did you say?' asked Morag.

'I said she needs her bumps reading. I mean, her head seeing to,' I explained, seeing that she was not familiar with the expression.

'A good dose of castor oil is what we always give them here, mo ghaoil,' she said simply. 'A girl or two hereabouts has got that way sometimes, but a good dose of castor oil works it out of them quicker than anythin'.'

Hector came in to the kitchen, sidled up to me and slapped my behind. 'Tsere's one of tsese hikers outside,' he told me, having thus ensured my attention. 'He's wantin' to know will you find him a bed for tse night?'

Immediately I suspected a joke. A stranded hiker on Christmas Day in Bruach was too unlikely.

'Why did he come here?' I asked.

'He says he couldn't see any lights any place else.'

Erchy shouldered his way in. 'Here, it's startin' to snow,' he said, 'and there's a fellow outside says he's stranded. Come out here and talk to him.'

I pretended to agree and went with him to the door. Outside stood a solitary figure huddled into a waterproof cape. A cap was pulled well down over his eyes and he had an enormous bundle on his back. The voice that addressed me was ripe Glaswegian. Dugan, I knew, was an excellent mimic of the Glaswegian accent. I darted at the figure and, exclaiming contemptuously, snatched off his cap and dragged him forward. 'Come along,' I told him. 'You don't fool me.' He hung back, so laughingly I went behind and prodded him forcibly. Inside the lighted kitchen the figure stood shivering with, I hoped, cold, for I realized that he was a complete stranger. Erchy and Hector looked at me as though I had gone mad. Morag and Behag stopped with their knives poised and waited for an explanation. The situation hardly improved when I began to shake with laughter. 'I'm sorry,' I tried to explain, 'but I thought someone had dressed up for a joke. We're having a party here as I dare say you've guessed, and I just couldn't believe there'd really be anyone hiking to Bruach at this time of year and in such weather.'

The hiker's face thawed into a timid grin and after a plate of hot soup he seemed to accept that he had not fallen into such wild company as he must at first have suspected.

'I must go and see if I can get hold of Janet and ask her if she can give you a bed,' I said.

'Ach, put him in your own bed,' advised Erchy. 'Put a pillow between you and everythin' will be all right.'

The hiker's face resumed its hunted look.

Luckily, Janet had a spare bed and took the hiker off my hands. 'Thank God's my sister's away to her bed with the cold,' she murmured as she departed, 'his trousers are soaked through.' It was singularly unfortunate for the poor hiker that when Janet arrived home she found a party of her friends awaiting her. They had come, well provisioned, to begin celebrating the New Year. The hiker had gone off to bed, Janet told me later, but so noisy and so lengthy had been the ensuing celebration that it was doubtful if he managed a wink of sleep the night through. It was even more unfortunate that Janet had overslept the next morning and had not awakened until disturbed by the shouts of the hiker who was having a battle with Grace in the kitchen as to the ownership of the trousers he had left to dry there overnight.

'Indeed, my dear,' Janet said mournfully, 'I believe that's one man who'll never come within sight of this village again so long as he draws breath.'

Various whoops and bangs, interspersed by exuberant retchings of the melodeon, came from the direction of the shed. The dancing had obviously begun and Behag went to extricate Fiona from the throng so that Morag, who was not staying for the dancing, could take her home. It was already past eleven o'clock but the child showed no sign of fatigue. I pushed the kettles to the side of the fire and went to see how things were progressing. Dollac, who had been my staunchest supporter all through the preparations for the festivities, had hurried home to change into a party dress, promising faithfully to be back in time to help me and Behag serve the refreshments. I looked for her among the milling dancers but as yet she had not put in an appearance. The postman was playing the melodeon with a verve that was in some measure due to the bottle of whisky I had seen him furtively stuffing into the mailbag behind the tree. Some of the girls were teaching their partners to dance a St. Bernard's waltz, the tuition consisting of kicking their partners feet sharply until they were in the required positions. They had pulled sprigs of mistletoe from the bunch Mary had sent me and this they wore in their hair, but the men seemed to be uninterested or unaware of the implied invitation.

When the dancers paused there were complaints of thirst and after consulting with Behag I decided not to wait for Dollac's arrival but to serve the refreshments straight away.

'See and put a good tin of baking soda an' a spoon handy, so folks can help themselves,' Morag had warned before she left, and so I put a couple of pounds of it in a jar beside the tree and at frequent intervals the men resorted to it, swallowing down two or three heaped teaspoonfuls at a time. Naturally, they had all brought their bottles and every few minutes purposeful groups of them disappeared from the shed and came back each time looking a little live-

lier or a little sleepier, according as it affected them. The
night rushed on. At one time I noticed Shamus who apparently considered himself young enough for children's parties and old enough for adult ones, dancing an alternately
constrained and abandoned version of the Highland Fling
which brought much applause. There was a respite for song
and the roadman gave us one of his own composition. It
told the story of a hen who had taken herself off to a secret
nest where she had reared one chick—a cockerel. It was
wholly derogatory and brought screams of laughter.

Two o'clock came and there was still no sign of Dollac
and as I had never known her miss a rehearsal or indeed
any chance of entertainment, I started enquiring if anyone
knew why she had not returned to the dance.

'You'd best ask Adam,' said Elspeth, with a little secret
smile. 'I believe he knows why she's not here.'

I collared Adam on his way to an appointment with a
bottle. He was bubbling with fun and voluble with whisky
and he was only too ready to tell me what had happened to
Dollac.

'Well it's like this,' he began. 'Dollac promised she'd
come to the dance with Duncan, and Johnny didn't like
that at all. He thought she should come with him. Ach, you
know fine yourself how it's been with Dollac and Johnny
these three years back. I believe he's been wantin' her to
marry him for a good while but she won't just say that she
will.' As a matter of fact the relationship between Dollac
and Johnny had never appeared to me to be anything more
than platonic, but it seemed I was mistaken. 'Ach, he's crazy

about her right enough,' went on Adam. 'Indeed I'm hearin' he's after buyin' the ring a twelve month back and he's been takin' her old man buckets of fish heads for his creels for longer than that. Anyway, while she was out at the cows this afternoon what does Johnny do but climb in through her bedroom window and pinch all her clothes. Not a blessed thing did he leave her that she could wear for the dance. At least that's what she was tellin' me when I called in on my way here. You see, I had to nip up and put my mother to bed after the pantomime was finished,' he explained. 'Aye, but I felt sorry for Dollac, right enough. She's been lookin' forward to this dance more than anybody, and there she was sittin' beside the fire in her workin' clothes just like she was when she was Cinderella in the play,' Adam chuckled.

'Where is Johnny?' I cut in, looking in vain for him among the dancers. Duncan, seemingly unaffected by Dollac's desertion, was capering friskily through a 'Dashing White Sergeant'.

'I expect he's at home, keepin' guard over Dollac's clothes,' said Adam. 'He was here at the pantomime, but he went home when Dollac did.'

It was past four o'clock in the morning and I was yawning undisguisedly, hoping to infect some of my spirited guests with a little of my own weariness, when the door was suddenly flung back and Johnny and Dollac stood on the threshold, grinning self-consciously at us all. Johnny's eyes were glittering and he was brandishing a full bottle of whisky, inviting everyone to 'come and celebrate', an invitation to which Duncan responded with even more alacrity than the rest. Dollac was wearing a sea-green dress that had been depicted on the front page of the most recent mail-order catalogue and captioned 'For Allure with a capital A'. The colour endowed her with a naiadic beauty so that it was not difficult to imagine she had swirled in on a cloud of spray.

'What are you celebratin',' called Adam. 'Is it just that you've gathered in the last of your hay today or it is because you've gathered in Dollac at last?'

'Both,' retorted Johnny, with a flash of assertiveness, and with an enraptured look at Dollac he seized her left hand and held it up for us to see the diamond sparkling on the third finger.

We congratulated, we hugged, we cheered and admired. The melodeon blossomed again into a 'Strip the Willow' for which Dollac and Johnny led off. Heaven alone knew now what time the party would end.

'Hell!' came Erchy's muzzy voice in my ear, 'the way I'm feelin' now I think I must have been a bit in love with Dollac myself.'

Vocabulary

Cailleach	*old woman*
Bodach	*old man*
Cas Chrom	*the old Hebridean foot-plough*
Pliach	*a rough home-made dibber for planting potatoes*
Mo ghaoil	*my dear*
Skart	*the shag, or green cormorant*